Plant Marriages

Plant Marriages

Jeff Cox

*What Plants Look Good Together ~ How to Choose the
Perfect Plant Combinations for Your Garden*

HarperCollins*Publishers*

For Pat and Clare

Library of Congress Cataloging-in-Publication Data

Cox, Jeff, 1940–
      Plant marriages : what plants look good together : how to choose the perfect plant combinations for your garden / Jeff Cox. — 1st ed.
           p.   cm.
      Includes bibliographical references and index.
      ISBN 0-06-016818-8
      1. Landscape gardening. 2. Plants, Ornamental. 3. Gardens—Design.
   I. Title.
   SB473.C692 1993
   712'.6—dc20   92-53354
                                                                                    CIP

Printed in Singapore
First Edition
10 9 8 7 6 5 4 3 2 1

Edited by Charles A. de Kay
Designed by Dirk Kaufman
Produced by Smallwood and Stewart, New York City

CONTENTS

INTRODUCTION

The Plant Marriage

When most of us first enter a beautiful garden, our impression is not so much of individual plants, but of their artful arrangement in the landscape. But, if we take some time to look around, we begin to notice that the garden succeeds because certain plants really look wonderful together. This is no accident. Carefully conceived, the smaller groupings that highlight the whole, or what I call "marriages," are the gifts of gardeners to lovers of beauty.

To anyone trying to "marry" plants in the garden, however, the question always comes back to this: What looks right with what, and will those plants grow well together?

There is no one answer, but, to my mind, a good marriage is any simple combination of two, three, or even four individual plants that complement each other. One must bring together mates that enhance the others' features and create a grouping that is more beautiful than the plants would be on their own.

Of course, virtually any plants can be grouped, but not all make happy marriages. I've seen red annual salvia (*Salvia coccinea*) paired with zinnias, for instance, so many times it seems a cliché; to my eye, this unflattering match just lumps color together in a manner that is neither artful nor subtle. In general, I think the same is all too often true of many traditional beds and borders, where plants are usually massed, somewhat indiscriminately, into large areas of color. A good plant marriage would bring special splashes of beauty to those same beds and borders, enhancing them with smaller and more interesting areas of color and texture.

As the following pages will demonstrate, making good marriages requires some creative thinking. But, surprisingly, it really does not take extra work, because the steps are the same in planting any garden: you must evaluate your site, consider the environmental needs of the individual plants you want to feature, and plan ahead to different seasons and how plants will look in various stages of maturity.

Fortunately, no spot is too small for a good marriage; think of how lovely two ideal mates—erigeron and violets, for instance—look in a planter or windowbox. Indeed, if the match

The pinkish mauve-lavender flowerheads of Sedum *'Autumn Joy' make a subtle color marriage with the blue-purple flowers of* Aster amellus *'King George'. Shown here in August, by late September the sedum flowers will turn a deep reddish-burgundy color and still look good with the last of the asters.*

is good, any plant marriage will be beautiful. Potting plants is only one possibility; in a mixed border beautiful marriages can also be set off to great effect by neutral foliage or inconspicuous plants, or featured as centerpieces in island beds.

No matter where you put the plants, experimentation is an important part of the process, as it is not always predictable which plants will look better together than alone. I find it helps to carry a new plant around my yard to see how it looks against other plantings. I once did this with a large clump of rose fountain grass (*Pennisetum alopecuroides*) until I discovered that it looked beautiful beneath a small stand of glossy, dark-leaved holly (*Ilex aquifolium 'Teufel's Deluxe'*) growing by my house. Once I saw them together, their lovely contrasts were obvious; the grass was light and soft-textured, the holly dark, hard, and prickly. Yet I would not have thought of this marriage without actually seeing those two plants next to each other.

Do not be disappointed if your first idea does not turn out to be the best. Plants are easily moved when they are young—except for tap-rooted plants, which resent having their roots disturbed. If a combination does not work out the way you hoped pretty quickly, break it up and try another. Chances are, it will not get better with time.

Above all, remember that your garden should please you. There are no hard-and-fast rules for marrying plants. Meant to inspire, this book offers guidelines, not dictums. Once you have tried a few new marriages in your garden, and begin to see what works and why, you will develop your own sense of style. In the meantime, enjoy the process of discovery.

Unlike perennial flower color which comes and too quickly goes, pretty foliage marriages stay all season. Here the light yellow-green grasslike leaves of Hakonechloa macra *'Aureola' are heightened in drama by the highly contrasting dark green leaves of* Viburnum davidii *on the left.*

CHAPTER ONE

THE ELEMENTS OF PLANT COMPATIBILITY

The first step in creating a successful plant marriage is to study the plants you are planning to feature in your garden. Consider the specific attributes of each plant: the flower color, the overall shape, and its habit. Are the blossoms pleasing to you? Are there ornamental seedpods and fruits? Is there anything about the leaf color, size, and shape, or even such details as bark texture that catches your eye? What is it about them that especially appeals to you? Identify these qualities, and it will then be much easier to choose compatible mates that will highlight their attractive characteristics.

If, for example, you decide that the primary elements of your combination are flower shape and color, then think about partners that will enhance those characteristics. But also consider how the plant's secondary characteristics—perhaps leaf texture or shape—will affect the grouping. With a fringe tree (*Chionanthus virginicus*) the primary feature is its puffy white flowers, for example. For a good match, you might try the butterfly bush (*Buddleia davidii*), whose purple panicles set off the white fringe-tree flowers while remaining distinct. Then highlight the secondary features of the butterfly bush—its graceful gray-green leaves—include a tree with contrasting foliage, such as the bronze leaves of a dwarf peach tree.

Plants can be made to enhance each other through the use of contrast, repetition, or affinity. Of these three techniques, con-

Dark plants are generally highlighted by a lighter backdrop, and light plants by a dark one. Here Malus 'Profusion' is opening its smoldering red-pink buds against a white-flowered prunus.

trast produces the most drama, because the differences in the partners call attention to the individual character of each. For example, the small, busy leaves of a boxwood would disappear if the plant was paired with another small-leaved shrub like cotoneaster, but the same foliage is vibrant against a large-leafed plant like a hosta. Contrasts can also be made in color, texture, plant form, and scale, as well as in leaf shape and size.

Repeating a color from one flower to another is a good means of marrying plants. Some flower blossoms contain more than one color, and thus have their own built-in complementary or harmonizing color accents; good examples are multi-colored Johnny-jump-ups and dark blue-purple delphinium florets, which have bright yellow "bees" at their centers. These natural variegations are excellent starting points for choosing a partner. Or you might echo a distinctive form, such as in a pairing of mounded plants like gray-green nepeta and purple sage (*Salvia leucophylla*). Their habits make them work well together, while their different colors save the marriage from being dull.

Plants also pair well if they are related through affinity, meaning that their colors, shapes, or textures mix well because they are similar but not identical. The puffy white flowers of baby's-breath (*Gypsophila paniculata*), for instance, look beautiful with the puffy mauve flowers of the smoke tree (*Cotinus coggygria*), yet they remain visually separate because of the difference in colors.

The best overall approach to plant marriages is simplicity. Generally a basic, simple grouping will catch the eye and hold it far more effectively than a complicated arrangement that will overwhelm the viewer; an effective, simple marriage will be compelling enough to stand on its own, yet will also work well in a larger design scheme.

Color

When asked, most gardeners will say that color is their first concern; they want lots of it to brighten up their gardens—and who can blame them? The fresh, lively hues of flowers delight the eye and lift the spirits. What a dim, cheerless place the world would be without them!

Traditionally, gardeners have used color for a general decorative effect—as in a cottage garden, where helter-skelter arrangements turn into brilliant mixes of overall color, or in a typical walkway border, where rows of petunias or marigolds create a bold edge. But color principles can also be applied to smaller plant groupings. In fact, color is the primary feature of most plant marriages. It is the attribute we are apt to notice first and has the greatest impact on a grouping.

Pairing plants of the same color is a logical, natural way to link them, and helps highlight disparate flower shapes. In a monochromatic scheme of white foxgloves (*Digitalis purpurea* 'Alba') and white roses, for example, the contrast in the two different flower forms will be more visible than if they had been different colors.

Indeed, some very effective marriages are made with plants of the same color, or more typically, of harmonizing shades of the same color (see box on this page). In a marriage based on yellow, for instance, the bright lemon-yellow of lemon daylilies (*Hemerocallis lilio-asphodelus*) works well with the deep golden-orange hue of 'Starburst Orange' daylillies, the gorgeous creamy yellow of 'Cobham Gold' Shasta daisies, and the accents in a broad-leafed, yellow-edged hosta.

Understanding why different plants harmonize means understanding some basic color principles. Within each color is an infinite variety of shades that vary according to hue, intensity, and value. Hue is the pure color: red, blue, green, mauve, and so forth, intensity is how saturated the color is—from the palest pastel to the deepest concentrated color—and value is the degree of light and dark in the color.

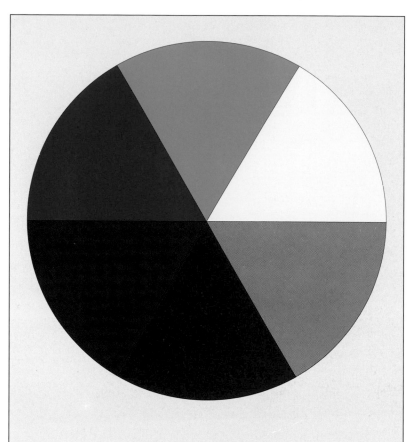

The Color Wheel

The color spectrum is usually thought of as a wheel, in which all color is divided into three types—primary, secondary, and tertiary.

The primary colors—those which cannot be produced by mixing any other color—are red, yellow, and blue. When equal parts of two primary colors are mixed, they yield the secondary colors: violet, green, and orange. The six tertiary colors are created when a primary color is mixed with its adjacent secondary hue.

Colors which are "harmonious" contain some portion of one another; the closer two colors are on the wheel, the better they will harmonize. The greatest contrast, on the other hand, is found in complementary colors, which are opposites on the color wheel and contain no part of one another. When placed side by side, complementary colors tend to "vibrate" and contrast strongly.

*Even though their forms are repetitive, the daisy-like flowers of the asters and the yellow-orange black-eyed Susans (*Rudbeckia fulgida*) make a good marriage, because of the severe color contrast.*

A good rule of thumb for relating plants through color is to use flowers of the same hue but different intensity—as in a pairing of the pastel, almost ghostly lemon-yellow *Coreopsis* 'Moonbeam' and the shrubby cinquefoil (*Potentilla fruticosa* 'Primrose Beauty'), which is a more saturated lemon-yellow. Varying both hue and intensity is trickier, but can be equally

Most of the garden is green for most of the year: that's the adage, and, as the photo opposite shows, the reality; so it is important to use off-colors and variegations to keep interest in the landscape. Varying shades of green and varying sizes and shapes of leaves, from the light green Queen Anne's lace to the dark green, large-leaved gunnera, make for a cool, restful and interesting picture, even when the garden is nearly all green. Here Hosta sieboldiana *'Frances Williams', with its yellow edges on dark green leaves marries well with the yellow leaves of* Ribes sanguineum *'Brocklebankii' and the small variegated leaves of* Weigela florida *'Variegata' at top.*

pleasing, as in the marriage of golden-orange flower balls of Japanese kerria (*Kerria japonica*) with the greenish yellow flower bracts of some types of spurge.

Value is ordinarily determined by the quality of light in your garden. Because color values change with every cloud that passes over the sun, and with the sun's daily (and seasonal) spin around the heavens, it is easier to watch these variations as they naturally occur than it is to arrange them. But if you want color in shady areas, or perhaps in a part of the garden where you like to walk in the evening light, it is helpful to know that blues and violets tend to stand out in low light, while reds will fade away.

Since light affects value, some color marriages are better suited to the east than to the west, and vice versa. Low-value and low-intensity colors, such as the pale pastel flowers of phlox (*Phlox paniculata*), for example, wash out under the glare of vigorous California sunlight and in the western Sunbelt regions; brighter, more saturated flowers like California poppies (*Eschscholzia californica*), with their rich buttery yellows, are a better choice for these areas. East of the Rockies, where cloud cover and dappled light are more typical—and where all colors tend to stand out better—pastels such as pale blue mertensia, the pastel yarrows, and pale pink bouncing bet (*Saponaria officinalis*) can be used to better advantage.

Beautiful and balanced plant marriages can also be made by accenting with complementary colors. A favorite approach of mine is to relieve a broad swath of color (and add "spice") with splashes of complementary hues. A bed of violets and lavender tulips, for instance, tucked into a mixed border of perennials and shrubs is attractive, but the marriage really comes to life when a contrasting touch of purest yellow is added, as in 'Basket of Gold' allysum.

An elegant color scheme is, I believe, made up of soft pastel shades with intense accent colors—as when soft pink 'P.J.M.' rhododendrons are planted in front of cherry plums (*Prunus cerasifera*), an accent plant distinguished by coppery red leaves. An all-white scheme, on the other hand, can produce a very formal look, as can a combination of evergreens.

As you begin to train your eye to plant marriages that seem

*When choosing color schemes, adding complementary colored accents such as the purple spikes of apple mint (*Mentha suaveolens*) with the yellow oregano (*Origanum vulgaris*), seen in the photo above, brings the main color to life. Yellows and red-oranges dominate the palette in fall and seem to be highlighted by the waning light at that time of year, as shown, left. On the opposite page, clear, strong red-orange colors are especially vibrant and eye-catching;* Lychnis coronaria *is the striking red-magenta flower, while* Alstroemeria aurantiaca *is the orange component.*

to work well, you will likely notice some color associations are more common than others. In general, I find that mauve and blue-gray harmonize with most colors and white goes with everything. Because complementary colors vibrate, use these contrasting combinations sparingly.

I also like burgundy and pink together, as well as clear, strong reds used with a lot of pale blue, as in Maltese-cross (*Lychnis chalcedonica*) combined with sage (*Salvia gregii*). In the end, your own taste is the one to satisfy. Do not be afraid to try some less commonly used combinations: brownish golds and oranges for example, or gray-greens with burgundies. As you get a better sense of what colors please you, you will also develop your own ways of using them.

Flowers

Coordinating flower color often overshadows all other considerations in designing a garden. This is understandable, as flowers are a garden's greatest ornamental asset. Since most perennials, with few exceptions, last for only part of a growing season, augmenting their numbers with annuals will extend the blooming period in your garden. Flower blossoms are particularly important in marriages that include annuals, as most annuals are not known for their distinguished foliage. If you want to use an annual to duplicate a perennial that has already bloomed in order to extend the life of a marriage, simply choose one with similar flower shape and color.

To make a great plant marriage with flowers, however, you

The pink-violet-lavender portion of the color spectrum is particularly lovely when plants with those colors are carefully selected to marry in form as well. *Above,* Clematis viticella *strikes the deep rose color, while the hybrid clematis 'Hagley Hybrid' gives a pure pink, and 'Etoile Violet' are the violet stars in the center. At left, mauve-violet violas and the violet flowers of* Clematis integrifolia *vary shapes but not color. Opposite, pink dahlias and red* Monarda didyma *above, lavender asters in the center, and dark violet heliotropes below make a cool marriage in a sunny border.*

Two plants with medium-sized leaves of the same color, texture, and shape have no distinguishing effect. The feathery leaves of fennel (*Foeniculum vulgare*) would be lost among fern fronds, for example. But match fennel with a smooth, broad-leafed bergenia plant and you will have a winning combination.

Nor should the role of color be underestimated; in fact, leaves display almost as many variations in color as do flowers. Within the green family alone, colors range in value from almost black to the palest of pales. Some plants, like grasses, lean toward yellow, while succulents are apt to be bluish. But leaves can also be pure golden yellow, white, red, burgundy, purple, orange, brown, buff and mauve.

Neutral shades of gray, white, and bluish-green hues, as well as "dusty" shades, are useful for breaking up large areas of green, as are more unusual foliage colors that range in hue, value and intensity, which can also enliven a traditional mixed border. Plants with very dark leaves, like common monkshood (*Aconitum napellus*), work especially well with the silvery gray of the popular mound-forming artemisia *Artemisia schmidtiana*, whose shape also makes a good marriage with the taller monkshood. I also find that yellow and gold, combined with white and yellow-greens, make a beautiful foliage composition. The reddish leaves of Japanese maples (*Acer japonicum*), European beech (*Fagus sylvatica*), and red-leaved plums are also especially lovely with green and gray.

Some plants, such as pieris and photinia, are red-leaved only in spring, and their red phase can be planned as a seasonal effect to set off a green or gray-leaved partner; a great spring combination in this color scheme is *Photinia fraseri* and the Lawson cypress (*Chamaecyparis lawsoniana* 'Pembury Blue'), a beautiful gray shrub.

Most people do not think of using foliage to create dramatic marriages, but when the leaves are variegated or an unusual color, they can be highlighted in some stunning combinations. When you plant variegated houttuynia (*Houttuynia cordata* 'Chameleon'), which has a blend of pinkish red and yellow on its ivylike leaves, in the shade with Japanese anemones (*Anemone × hybrida*) and perhaps a white-and-yellow 'Wadda's

Primrose' clematis, the results are exquisite.

To my eye, one of the most exceptional foliage plants is the climbing ornamental kiwi (*Actinidia kolomikto*), with its variegated pink, green, and white leaves. There are just such colors in certain peonies, which bloom when the kiwi leaves variegate in the full June sun and make a wonderful partner for this plant. Ornamental kiwi is originally an east Asian plant; this always seems visible in its appearance, and its combination with the very Chinese-looking peonies seems to me to be close to perfect.

Form and Habit

I define "form" as the overall shape or profile of a plant, whether it is conical, rounded, mounded, chunky, or boxlike; and "habit" as the way a plant displays or carries itself. A plant's habit could be upright or weeping; tuft-forming or branching; climbing or prostrate; or dense or airy.

Form and habit are key attributes in plant marriages; they are particularly important when pairing trees and shrubs, which depend on the illusion of movement and balance for a good marriage. Wide, spreading shrubs look well-balanced when planted with tall, conical, or cylindrical evergreens. Forsythia and small trees such as Norway spruces (*Picea abies* 'Nidiformis') work well with Chinese juniper (*Juniperus chinensis*) cultivars; and dwarf white spruces (*Picea glauca* 'Conica') go well with upright deciduous trees like amelanchier and locusts.

Because of their size and distinctive form, certain plants—such as flowering crabapples, Japanese maples, and winged euonymus (*Euonymus alata*)—look best if only one plant is used, in a marriage or as a specimen planting. Others—such as azaleas, delphiniums, foxgloves, and most other upright perennials as well as most annuals—look attractive in small groups of three to seven plants. When in dout, use fewer rather than more plants in the marriage to keep the association simple.

I think of plants with distinctive forms as dance partners. I once

Opposite, a marriage of multi-hued evergreens with widely varied shapes which only highlight their subtle differences in color.

planted two young Japanese plums (different *Prunus salicina* cultivars) in my backyard without a firm sense of how they would eventually look together. As time passed, one grew tall and very upright; the other spread its limbs wide and low to the ground. The tall tree danced *en pointe*, while the lower one bowed with a sweep of its limbs. To my surprise and delight, they matured into a magnificent, balanced pairing.

As with any dance partner, grace is an asset. Many deciduous trees, including hawthorns, some crabapples, and numerous cherries and plums, display a delightfully strong but sinuous look of hard wood under smooth bark, as well as a sensuousness in the way their limbs resemble flexed muscles as they turn up and out to display their leaves.

The sculptural qualities of tree limbs are best seen after their foliage has fallen; therefore, marriages of trees should be designed in the winter. Soft evergreens, such as the Hinoki cypress (*Chamaecyparis obtusa* 'Gracilis'), make a fine foil for the bare structure of deciduous trees, while pendulous plants, like weeping willows (*Salix × babylonica*), are excellent winter partners for stiff, upright trees like black pines (*Pinus thunbergiana*).

Form and habit are also key factors in marrying herbaceous plants. While the stems of these plants tend to be straight, and generally do not have the strong, distinctive character of tree limbs and trunks, they, too, have interesting growth habits. Some are single-stemmed, like yarrows, foxgloves and

A marvelously shaped Prunus subhirtella *'Pendula Rosa', above, is set as a single specimen in a bed of snowdrops and winter aconites. This marriage is admirable before the tree flowers when its shape can be seen, and exquisite when the tree is in bloom.*

lilies, but many are multi-branched, including meadowsweet, Shasta daisies, lilies, and artemisias. Still others—daylilies, hostas, and agapanthus, for example—do not have stems at all, producing instead elegant scapes when the flowers are ready to blossom.

The overall shape of herbaceous plants and their inflorescences, or arrangements of floral elements on the stems, can really contribute to a grouping. Epimediums, for instance, have a tiered, off-center form that consorts nicely with a low, busy groundcover like mazus (*Mazus reptans*), while loose misty sprays of baby's-breath (*Gypsophila paniculata*) will beautifully set off stiff, clustered bellflowers (*Campanula glomerata*). Grasses and plants with tall, pendulous stems, such as fairy wand (*Dierama pulcherrimum*), are very useful to pair with low-growing mounds of herbaceous perennials or annuals, like globeflower (*Trollius* spp.), eupatorium, sedum, and marigolds. The grasses' curved leaves and stems contrast with the vertical forms of most other herbaceous plants, bringing grace and softness to a marriage.

Vines and climbing plants are too seldom used in plant combinations. Vines can be trained or coaxed to do a gardener's will and are wonderful mates for trees and tall shrubs. Clematis, growing up through 'Dortmund' shrub rose, will provide a double show as the two plants flower simultaneously. In my own garden, a Lady Bank's rose grows up into a pear tree for a progression of color. In spring, the rose showers creamy yellow flowers out of the tree; these are followed by white pear flowers, which in turn give way to the fruit, which ripens in August. The plants grow right beside the driveway, so the combination is one we frequently see and enjoy.

Fruits and Seedpods

Because their unusual shapes and rich, changing colors never fail to catch the eye, fruits and seedpods are particularly exciting additions to a marriage.

While fruits and seedpods are very attractive when combined with handsome foliage plants, caution should be exercised when associating them with equally showy flowers, because too much color can detract from the spectacle of the fruit. Similarly, pairing two berried specimens may result in a busy mass of dots. Combining the red-orange seedpods of a plant like American bittersweet (*Celastrus scandens*), for example, with the orange hips of *Rosa rubrifolia* would definitely be overkill. Yet, if the same bittersweet were to be planted behind the straight, vertical swords a yucca, the seedpods would seem appealing splashes of color in an artful composition.

Although fruits and seedpods—especially the very ornamental varieties such as cattails (*Typha* spp.), teasel, love-in-a-mist (*Nigella damascena*), and lunaria—can be spectacular, they are often short-lived, particularly if they appeal to birds. If this is the case in your garden, base your combination on other attributes of the plant and let their fruit or pods be an added attraction.

There are many plants whose fruits hang long into winter, including hawthorns, distinguished by clusters of red fruit; cotoneasters and pyracanthas, with their masses of showy red berries; and many crabapples, whose hard little fruits last well beyond fall. In warmer climates, persimmons and citrus fruits will provide sustained interest.

Seasonal Impressions

The larger landscape has a distinct appearance in each season, even in warmer regions of the country. Most plants also change in character with the seasons as they gain and lose their leaves, flowers, and fruits. As plants fade, so will marriages, if the peak growing months of their partners are too similar.

Of course, plant marriages can be made for strictly seasonal displays, but as one partner changes—drops its leaves, for example—new characteristics may emerge that you want to emphasize. Birch trees, for instance, have beautiful bark that can be set off with a late-winter flowering plant, such as a camellia or witch hazel, making a handsome marriage before the tree comes into leaf in spring.

Marriages planted in the garden can be designed so that they have something of beauty to offer all year long. Following are some ideas:

The Joys of Spring

"Nature's first green is gold, her hardest hue to hold," wrote Robert Frost. Indeed, it is true that when new leaves appear in the spring, they often look golden in the sunlight, casting a greenish gold haze over the landscape. But as the poet suggests, this impression is fleeting. Consider it a fringe benefit and do not plan your garden around it.

Perhaps because it is so evanescent, spring is possibly the most dramatic season, a time when woody plants come into leaf and flowers bloom with the first vibrant colors that are so welcome after the monotonous hues of winter. I particularly notice trees in spring. I like the look of blossoms against branches as trees burst into flower before their leaves come out, and I try for this effect in certain plant marriages. Trees and shrubs that flower before the leaves appear benefit from a background of dark evergreens.

Call attention to the branches of a specimen tree in early spring by making a marriage with colorful bulb plants. One of my favorite sights at this time of year is the curving branches of devilweed (*Osmanthus delavayi*) or a deutzia (*Deutzia × elegantissima*) emerging from a bed of rich blue Siberian squill (*Scilla siberica*) mixed with delicate blue-and-white glory-of-the-snow (*Chionodoxa luciliae*).

Summer Glories

Summer sun is strong and penetrating. Plants in the sun seem to flare with light, while those in the shade go dark by contrast. Almost all sun-loving trees, shrubs, vines, perennials, and annuals peak in this season, offering weeks of drama and dazzling color.

Sunlight affects the way we see foliage as well as flower colors in the summertime. The summer sun can dissolve the subtleties in colors and textures. Some leaves are translucent; when the

The flowers and seedheads of many herbaceous perennials are still attractive after the first killing frost. A marriage of frost-covered border plants, opposite, enhances the fall landscape.

sun shines on them, they will turn an almost fluorescent green or red, as with Japanese maples (*Acer japonicum*) and black locusts (*Robinia pseudoacacia*).

On hot summer days, the shady areas of your garden are especially inviting, so be sure to feature some marriages where you can enjoy them as you relax in a cool spot. For example, a summertime marriage of black snakeroot (*Cimicifuga racemosa*), a plant with dramatic vertical white flowers, and cool blue, crested gentians (*Gentiana septemfida*), with their pretty trailing foliage and trumpetlike blossoms, will bring refreshing color to a shady area.

Fall Displays

Color on fire comes to mind for this time of year. I think it is best to forget about making delicate marriages in cooler regions of the country in the autumn, as they will get lost against the backdrop of brilliant hues that run riot in the landscape. Instead, try putting trees and shrubs together that will put on a show as their own leaves turn. A sweetgum (*Liquidambar styraciflua*) surrounded by sassafras (*Sassafras albidum*) and a sumac (*Rhus aromatica*), and entwined with Virginia creeper (*Parthenocissus quinquefolia*), will yield a spectacular fall fireworks display after frost has hit.

Colorful leaves are not the only consideration. When making autumn plant associations, keep late-flowering varieties in mind as well; the Franklin tree (*Franklinia alatamaha*), common witch hazel (*Hamamelis virginiana*), asters, Autumn crocus (*Colchicum autumnale*), and goldenrod (*Solidago canadensis*) are particular fall favorites.

Winter Expressions

The dead of winter—those endless weeks between Christmas and March—seems dreary no matter what part of the country you live in. But this is the time of year that needled and broadleafed evergreens come into their own. Think of how starkly beautiful deciduous tree limbs are when shown off against these dark evergreens, accented, perhaps, with winter fruiting shrubs like cotoneasters and barberries.

Winter marriages can be just as remarkable as other seasonal combinations. Some plants, such as the Harry Lauder's walking stick (*Corylus avellana* 'Contorta'), which has fantastically twisted, corkscrewlike branches, may actually look better when their leaves have fallen. I also favor trees with richly colored bark for winter groupings, including shrubby Siberian dogwoods (*Cornus alba* 'Sibirica'), which are bright red, as well as golden and black bamboos (*Phyllostachys* spp.), sycamores, and the pretty gray-barked American beech (*Fagus grandifolia*).

A plant with interesting bark is best set off against a background of evergreens. White birches (*Betula papyrifera*) are striking when silhouetted by dark green, while the reddish bark of an Amur cherry (*Prunus maackii*) or a paperbark maple (*Acer griseum*) might benefit more from the lighter green background of cedars or junipers.

In many regions, garden-viewing is done from the house, or at least from the porch, during cold months. When you are planning winter combinations, think about that view when it is at its dullest, and try to pick up the scene with a striking winter marriage. You may even want to place a floodlight in a judicious spot; a garden has a peculiarly beautiful and sadly romantic quality when light picks up the swirling snow at night.

Remember, as well, that there are also good possibilities for warm climates: red primroses and cyclamens, for example, are both winter bloomers, and will bring color to southern gardens during winter months.

Growth and Maturity

Plants change in shape, size, and posture as they journey toward maturity. Some plants, among them junipers and certain eucalyptuses and acacias, actually have very different leaves during different stages of their lives. And when English ivy (*Hedera helix*) reaches maturity, it takes on a completely new form, growing more like a bush than a vine.

Thus, an association that works well when two plants are young may not succeed at all when they are older. Planting a low-growing shrub like cinquefoil with a young crape myrtle (*Lagerstroemia indica*) may be fine for a few years, but when the crape myrtle reaches 20 feet tall and spreads 15 feet wide, the sun-loving cinquefoil will be thrown into shade and swallowed up by its more dominant partner.

Since plants are at maturity for the longest portion of their lives, it is best to devise the marriage for that stage. This means allowing two or three years for herbaceous perennials, three to five years for woody shrubs, climbers and vines, and eight to ten years for trees for the marriage to reach its peak.

It may be easier to coordinate plants that reach about the same size at maturity—even different cultivars of the same species—but try to keep some variation in size so the effect is not awkward. A mix of different holly shrubs, for example, with varied leaf colors, from bright yellow to blue-green to dark almost black-green, can be effective, but can also become boring after a while because the variations of size and form are so limited. Changing scale of leaf size, or better still, plant size, adds a more dynamic element to the marriage. A good rule of thumb is to scale the smaller of the marriage partners to at least a third the size of the larger ones.

Plants tend to grow quickly at first, then slow down after they reach early maturity. During the early phase of rapid growth, limit your pruning and cutting. When growth slows and plants have reached maturity, keep them in bounds by dividing, pruning, and thinning. Pruning and thinning are especially important to vines and climbers. Wisteria, for example, can grow to an enormous size over the years if left alone, and will easily overwhelm other plants in a marriage.

Trees, too, may eventually outgrow a plant marriage with smaller shrubs or herbaceous plants. If this happens, you may want to take the marriage apart and consider the tree as a candidate for a new pairing with other larger, woody plants.

The bold red twigs of Salix alba *'Chermesina' make a strong winter marriage with the gorgeous bluish-green evergreen Lawson cypress (*Chamaecyparus lawsoniana *'Pembury Blue'), with its scale-like leaves , opposite.*

CHAPTER TWO

DESIGNING WITH PLANT MARRIAGES

While each plant marriage is an individual work of beauty and should be positioned to stand out in the landscape, it must still relate to its surroundings. Large landscapes best accommodate simple, bold marriages that can be seen from a distance, particularly when they are repeated throughout as a unified composition. Intricate, delicate associations, however, need close-up viewing and fit better into smaller spaces. A gardener with just a bit of room to work in might still insert drama with a small grouping such as a miniature, orange-red rose paired with *Ophiopogon nigrescens*, an almost black, grasslike plant.

Consider first the big picture when planning the garden, then turn to the smaller details. If you are starting from scratch, begin with the major landscaping elements—fences and walkways, lawn areas, flower and vegetable beds—that will form the framework of your design. Once these are in place, a careful survey will help reveal what sites are suitable for marriages of different sizes and cultural needs. It is not possible to have too many plant marriages as long as they are well situated.

Whether your garden is new or established, first determine the position or angle from which your featured combinations will most often be seen. Begin at your house. Are there picture

An unsurpassed plant marriage for spring: The single white blooms of a cherry tree provide a dramatic canopy for a bed of tulips. Echoing the color of the blooms above, white and yellow tulips also serve to diffuse the hot color of the surrounding plantings.

windows? Is there a patio, deck, porch, or balcony from which you can view plants? Then: Where do you spend the most time outdoors? What places can be seen easily from there?

Next, walk around your yard, and note the spots where your eye falls naturally—areas that beg for special treatment. These might be atop a knoll, between a rock and a tree, at the bend of a path, or where that same path cuts through a hedge or wall. A view framed by foliage, fences, or walls also naturally attracts attention, and is a wonderful spot for a marriage.

Quite simply, wherever the landscaping carries your eye naturally will likely offer a good spot for a marriage (see box, page 32). Seen from 100 feet away, a garden will have one (or even several) natural focal points; these points are the right places to group large trees and shrubs. As you move in closer, the scene will draw your eye to newer, smaller places that were not visible before. Those visible from 30 feet away will suit small trees and shrubs, very large perennials, or drifts of 2- to 3-foot-high perennials, while any ten feet in or closer will show off small shrubs, perennials and annuals, and groundcovers to advantage.

While siting your marriages at focal points is critical, you do not want them to stand out like sore thumbs in the landscape. Set off a featured grouping against neutral or green surroundings—either with quiet plantings or mulch (see below).

Although the English gardening concept of interlocking drifts, where one large mass of color joins another, is and always will be a good one, I think an artful combination of extraordinarily good marriages is far more effective. Repeat marriages in a bed or border down the line of composition, separating them by whites or neutral gray or green foliage plants or with other subtle, complementary marriages.

In short, try to avoid the ordinary, or combinations that are hackneyed from overuse. The pitfall of cliché is well illustrated by traditional foundation plantings, such as masses of evergreen shrubs along the base of a house. The usual clumps of yews are particularly uninspired, but plants are still necessary to soften the foundation of a building and tie it to the ground. For a more imaginative approach, try breaking up the house line with a series of good plant marriages, such as Chinese blue column junipers paired with greener pfitzer junipers. These have a harmony of needle foliage and their colors mingle nicely. Why not plant some shrubs that yield fruit—plants like blueberries, currants, or bush cherries— along the foundation? They will cover the foundation, and provide seasonal treats.

Fill Space Well

Once you have decided on a site, put in a plant marriage— or a group of marriages—that is appropriate in scale. The width of the site should include room for surrounding plants and other elements, such as large rocks or pathways that will separate it from the rest of the landscape; and the width of the arrangement should measure roughly half to two-thirds the distance from which you anticipate it will be seen. Thus, combinations viewed from 30 feet away should be about 15 to 20 feet across.

You can also use this formula in reverse. For instance, if you have already planted a marriage that you estimate will take up six to eight feet in width, the optimum viewing point would be about 12 feet away, and would be the right place for a bench.

The recommended depth of a grouping depends on the individual plants you have chosen for the marriage, and on whether you are planting a backdrop, as in a hedge or row of evergreens behind a group of perennials. The higher your vantage point, the farther back your eye will be able to see. Bulky plants generally look better behind delicate varieties, as, of course, do taller ones.

Finding the Focal Points in a Landscape

In any good painting or sculpture, lines, shapes, and colors draw the eye to one inevitable place: the focal point. This is often where an action takes place, a color is emphasized, or a striking shape emerges. You can use the same design principle to help you decide where to place the plant marriages in your garden so they will attract the most attention.

To find the natural focal points in your yard, stand at key vantage points—a porch, driveway, or garden seat—and study the view directly in front of you; your sightline will take in a 90-degree angle, or one quadrant of an imaginary circle. Within this quadrant, look for strong "lines" that carry your eye from one place to another. These tend to show up most prominently in the trunks and branches of trees, and along pathways, shrublines, and lawn edges. Where the lines intersect, this is the focal point, (especially if three or more lines meet at that spot).

Diagonal lines are particularly important because they infer movement in the scene, and pull disparate elements together. Strong vertical and horizontal lines, on the other hand, tend to be static, breaking up a scene into parts, although they too draw the eye to a specific place, albeit with less vigor than horizontal lines.

Providing a Neutral Frame

The more striking the contrast between partners in a marriage, the more that marriage needs neutral surroundings to throw it into relief. Striking contrasts are meant to leap out visually to the viewer, but if the marriage is mixed with plants that detract attention from the partners—colorful perennials, for example—the impact of the marriage will be lost. Subtle marriages, on the other hand, can blend more with their site; bleeding hearts (*Dicentra spectabilis*) and Jacob's-ladder (*Palemonium caeruleum*) might be planted among the ferny leaves of an existing drift of astilbes. But surroundings should always set off the grouping, even if only in the quiet way this one does.

If the plantings adjacent to your site are going to compete with a marriage, choose another site or cut back the scene-stealers. Remove competing plants and replace them with less ostentatious ones, or with rocks.

In fact, rocks, along with trees and shrubs, work well to define and separate the various planting areas for marriages.

Large rocks are an important part of the "bony" structure of a landscape design. Not only can they separate areas (while bringing interest to flat, featureless terrain), they can also provide a sense of weight and mass to a garden.

Neutral trees and shrubs that do not call much attention to themselves include such plants as pines, barberries, cotoneasters, laurels, willows, hemlocks, privets, and viburnums. Use these to form screens and hedges, to provide settings or frameworks for marriages.

Some herbaceous perennials, among them ferns, pachysandra (*Pachysandra terminalis*), hostas, and hellebores, make good neutral foils as well. Hellebores grow in dark masses of evergreen foliage, and since they bloom in winter or very early spring, their pale flowers are not apt to clash with other marriages. Mulches, paving material, and some colored groundcovers such as ophiopogon, ajuga, and succulents can also help relieve the constant green of plant upon plant. Even in a small backyard garden, nothing but green is nothing but boring.

Garden Additions

Many designers think that a properly proportioned garden consists of one third plantings, one third ground area (including soil and lawns) and one third structural elements. Such "architectural" features, including paths, walls, arbors, and steps, help organize the landscape and frame settings in which plant marriages can be shown to best advantage. Other additions, like pools and planters, provide character and detail to a composition.

Terraces, Berms, and Stages

If your garden has unusual land contours, such as terraced levels, berms, or stages, make the most of them. Terraced levels, in particular, are visually compelling; their flat areas, which give a somewhat formal impression, make natural planting sites, while the vertical faces of their retaining walls provide places for plants to hang down or tumble over.

The highly defined beds of terraced levels demand a good overall design. I recommend massing herbaceous plants, such as a marriage of artemisias and rose campion (*Lychnis coronaria*); clustered bellflower (*Campanula glomerata*) and oxeyes (*Heliopsis*

spp.); or bee balm (*Monarda didyma*) and love-in-a-mist (*Nigella damascena*), an annual. Avoid woody plants (which will soon clutter up the neat appearance of the terrace), keep the height of your plant choices to about a third of the width of the bed, and stagger bloom times for interest as the seasons progress.

Berms, or long mounds of soil, may occur naturally in a landscape, but they are also often added to gardens to provide variation in a level expanse, create separate areas, edge a driveway, contain a pond, or to provide dry planting sites in an otherwise low-lying, soggy area. If you are installing a berm, bring in large rocks and boulders first, then put the soil on top of them. When the soil settles, the rocks will protrude here and there, and the whole effect will look more natural than if the rocks were stuck onto the outside.

To provide interest and create settings for several plant marriages, landscape berms with rocks and evergreens in a hide-and-reveal pattern, so that some areas of the base, slope, and top are visible and some hidden. Site the marriages in a similar hide-and-reveal manner so they are set off by the more neutral elements.

Groundcovers look good when their natural habit is emphasized and they are encouraged to spill down the sides of a berm and onto the flat ground below, tying the mound to its site. I have done this with ophiopogon, a grasslike perennial that likes shade, with bugleweed, and with succulents, again following the hide-and-reveal pattern. The groundcover flows as though it is being poured over the berm—running down in rivulets or wide streams, while not completely covering the area. If they contrast well enough, mix streams of groundcovers; the bright yellow-green licorice plant (*Helichrysum petiolatum* 'Limelight') and the dark green Irish moss (*Sagina subulata*), for instance, work well.

A stage, or raised, flat area surrounded by a low wall, is a great addition to the corner of a building where the walls intersect at an inward angle, and it is a perfect spot for a plant marriage. As a prominent feature, it calls attention to the plantings on it, giving them center stage. It looks especially good built out from a wall or border into the lawn, breaking up the predictable line of the grass edge. (If windows in the house look out onto the site, all the better.)

To keep a stage from looking boring, place the tallest plant or marriage toward the back, just slightly off-center, then add smaller shrubs or groupings of herbaceous plants around it so that their outlines "build up" to the taller, featured grouping. Put smaller herbaceous plants, groundcovers, or alpines around these, broken up toward the edge by larger shrubs (which can be used alone or in groups of two or three). This will break up the "volcano effect" that results from a numbingly regular advance from smallest plants on the outside up to the largest plant in the back.

Because a stage is elevated above ground level, it tends to dry out faster, and the plantings there will probably take

In the photo opposite, erigeron (Erigeron speciosus) tumbles down a set of steps, softening the hard stone edges, linking the change in level on the property, and associating with large-leaved plants behind it and on this side of the steps. Above, a marriage of red and pink geraniums (Pelargonium hybrids) achieve the same landscaping purposes.

more water than those in your yard. Make sure the soil in the stage is rich in humus, which will help hold water.

Walls

The separate forms of the individual plant partners are much more visible when arrayed against an attractive wall than in front of more greenery, where they may get lost. Whether painted or left untreated, wood surfaces provide uniform relief behind the busy leaves and blossoms, and all plants seem to look good next to stone, with its natural colorings.

A stone wall not only provides an elevated terrace for miniature flowering plant associations, but also creates places for specimens that tumble over the top, softening straight lines and sharp edges. Chinks between the rocks can hold those tough plants that look good even in such a "dry" environment; sedums and sempervivums are good examples.

If a wall is made of staggered rocks built into a berm or slope, it will provide lots of small planting areas for rock garden plants or alpines. Most of the familiar groundcovers, perennials, and some annual flowers are available in alpine forms—diminutive beauties to charm passersby. Plant marriages that you like in full size can often be reproduced in miniature using alpines: such as, a pincushion flower blooming above a mat of fine-leaved creeping veronica (*Veronica repens*).

I find that brick walls are among the nicest backdrops for plants. The regular brickwork patterns set off the sinuous forms of plants and leaves, while the bricks' dull red color shows off greens, whites, yellows, and pinks to great advantage.

In fact, the color of the wall is quite important. In addition to the subdued reds of brick, dull dark greens, blue-grays, ochres, and subtle shades of yellow all work well behind most plants. Soft paint colors—buffs, pale greens, and pale grays—also show off marriages, allowing the spotlight to remain on the plants.

Again, contrast is the key. Place dark foliage in front of lighter walls and light foliage in front of darker walls, and set off medium-colored varieties with very dark or very light walls. Try to avoid white; in sunny regions, white walls reflect too much

right in the water. A plant marriage viewed across an expanse of water has a double advantage: it has no competition from other plants, and it is reflected in the water. Light blue Japanese irises (*Iris kaempferi*) on the bank of a pond and red waterlilies in the water can look gorgeous together. For a truly exotic effect, try training passionflowers, roses, or wisteria on a trellis so they hang over a pool where lotuses are blooming.

Pathways

By defining the way you walk through a garden, pathways determine how plant arrangements will be viewed. The more paths twist and turn, revealing new sections as they go, for example, the more opportunities there are for featured plant combinations.

A turn in the path is an excellent place to display plant associations. If there is room, mass evergreens on one side of a path at a turn, and feature a marriage of herbaceous plants opposite. Other groupings can border the path along its length, but the turns are crucial: They guarantee attention because they require the walker to look down.

Entrances and exits, and any place where there is a change in the environment—as when the path passes under a shady canopy of trees from an area of full sun—are also good places for groupings, as are areas next to stairs, where passersby are apt to slow down. If a path is broad and level, plantings can be placed farther away, since those traveling them are more likely to look in the distance than if they are walking along a narrow, twisting walk.

I think a path looks best when bordering plants occasionally spill out onto it. Big clumps of ornamental grasses like pennisetum, miscanthus, or phormium are especially good choices for breaking up pathway lines, because of their tendency to

This marriage of full-size landscape plants is given a perfect setting: waterside so no plants interfere in the front, and the scene is reflected in the water. The twin plumes of pampas green (Cortaderia selloana) frame and define an entrance. The striking birches are Betula utilis. Notice the contrasts in color and form that help the eye keep the plants separate, yet look so pleasing as a whole.

lean out and interrupt the edges in interesting ways. Paths of large, flat rocks invite small marriages between the stones. An attractive match might be dark green and yellow-green mats of creeping thyme (*Thymus serphyllum*) paired with spiky, blue-gray mounds of pinks, which like full sun and gritty, lean soil. Thymes can take some foot traffic, as can mazus (*Mazus reptans*), a tiny plant with very interesting flowers; in the warmer areas, *Dichondra micrantha* is a good choice.

Plant Containers

Pots, urns, hanging baskets, window boxes, and other containers can turn plant combinations into eye-catching accents. Think of the pot in the same way you would an in-ground site—as a small arena for showing off a grouping that will stand out from its surroundings. Imagine red impatiens emerging from the pure blue flowers of lobelia, spilling its blossoms out over the edge of a large pot. Or a large clump of scilla tossing out its blue bells from amid dappled bits of light blue chionodoxa. An enormous terra-cotta pot placed next to a picket fence bordered by the large white and yellow flowers of Iceland poppies (*Papaver nudicaule*), in turn, looks wonderful filled with an elegant combination of the grayish white leaves of Crete dittany (*Origanum dictamnus*) and the small white and yellow flowers of snow-in-summer (*Cerastium tomentosum*), which appear over tiny whitish gray leaves. The snow-in-summer forms a whitish mat that tumbles gently over the edges of the pot, and the dittany throws out long arching stems with pretty little round leaves and lavender-flowering seedheads that look like bunches of hops.

When choosing containers, it is important to think about how the material will look with the plantings. Baskets make good neutral-colored homes for plantings; their texture provides added interest. For big pots and urns, I favor unglazed terra-cotta, which takes on a beautiful patina with time. Beware of glazed, white, or decorated pots, however, as a shiny bright surface or busy pattern may detract from the plants they contain. If a pot is noteworthy, feature it rather than the plants by planting it with something quiet—perhaps an evergreen—that does not detract from the showcase container.

CHAPTER THREE

A SEASONAL
PORTFOLIO

OF PLANT
MARRIAGES

SNOWDROPS & CROCUSES

Galanthus nivalis & *Crocus* hybrids

The Earliest Flowers Are the Most Welcome

Were snowdrops and crocuses to bloom in July, they would surely be lost amid the riotous colors and large, elaborate flower structures of midsummer. But because these small bulbs appear in March or April when all else is still dormant, the contrast of their fresh colors with the browns and grays of late winter could not be greater, nor their sight more welcome, so this marriage belongs in almost any garden.

Throughout the cold parts of the country, the first flower of the year is the common snowdrop (*Galanthus nivalis* 'Simplex'), which often blooms while snow is still on the ground—hence its name. As soon as the ground thaws, the snowdrop pushes its leaves upward, followed by a small, pure white droplet that appears from the tip of a central stalk. Eventually the outer three petals open like wings surrounding a shy, downward-facing, white flower tipped with bright green.

Soon the snowdrops are joined by crocuses with their extravagant lilacs, whites, yellows, creams, burgundies, and pur-

ples, each dotted with a cluster of bright orange stamens in their centers. The crocuses' Easter colors signify nature's wake-up call. Buds are swelling on some of the trees, and it will not be long before the grass greens, the leaves appear, and the world returns to vivid life.

To have more than a miniature effect, snowdrops should be planted in large numbers, and crocuses in only slightly smaller quantities. Both bulbs will naturalize if they like the spot, which they will if the soil is improved with humus-rich compost—especially the quickly spreading crocuses.

Because these bulbs bloom during the wet weather of early spring, plant them near to or along walkways or paths, beside the patio, around the house, or wherever they can be easily seen without a trek off into the mud. Snowdrops look especially good planted in the shade of rhododendrons or azaleas, or near dark evergreens, just to set them off. Both types of bulb will tolerate partial shade or full sun, so

White snowdrops dance for pure joy while crocuses herald the return of fresh spring smells and colors to the world.

SNOWDROPS & CROCUSES

	Zones	Height	Light	Soil	Highlights
Galanthus nivalis	4–9	6 in.	Sun to shade.	Rich, moist, woodsy soil.	Before the petals open, the flowers resemble pure white droplets.

Comments: This is the first flower to bloom. Be sure that your bulbs are commercially grown, not gathered from the wild.

	Zones	Height	Light	Soil	Highlights
Crocus hybrids	4–9	6 in.	Sun to shade.	Good garden soil.	Delicate cups in the colors of early spring, each with a central cluster of orange stamens.

Comments: Golden crocus (*Crocus chrysanthus*) is a species with many unusual colors that blooms even earlier than the hybrid forms.

they can also be planted in the open or under deciduous trees or shrubs.

I don't recommend planting bulbs in the lawn, however, as they require a spring's worth of sunlight to recharge the bulbs for next year's display. In most of the country, the grass tends to need cutting by April, which would shear off the bulb foliage while it is still needed to manufacture food for the bulbs. Instead, plant them in places where late-blooming perennials will arise, or where perennial

In the warmer zones, gardeners can interplant snowdrops—seen opposite in their droplet guise before their petals open—with winter bloomers like the Cyclamen coum *that bears pretty crimson-rose flowers resembling shooting stars. Above,* Cyclamen coum *blooms with* Crocus tomasinianus, *as early as January in Zones 9 and 10.*

groundcovers will emerge. The emerging foliage of the perennials will cover up the old bulb foliage as it turns brown.

Both types of bulbs should be planted in the fall in rich, moist, humus-rich, and well-drained soils. To create a bulb bed, remove the top four inches of soil from the area where the bulbs are to go. Take the box full of crocuses and toss them lightly across the bed to make a drift. Then place the snowdrop bulbs so they fill the areas where the crocuses didn't land thickly, creating intertwining drifts. Any bulbs less than three inches apart should be slightly repositioned so that they have at least three or four inches of room in which to grow, but try to maintain the general pattern of the bulbs as they fell. This gives a natural look to the interlaced drifts of bulbs. Turn all the bulbs upright so that their root end is

Other Very Early Spring Bulbs

While crocuses and snowdrops are among the earliest bloomers, there are several other bulbs that bloom around the same time or just slightly later. All of these are welcome, too, and are hardy to Zone 4.

Winter aconite (*Eranthis hyemalis*). Its yellow buttercup flowers appear above small-lobed leaves which are held horizontally, making the blossoms look as though they were sitting on a green ruff.

Siberian squill (*Scilla siberica*). Blooms slightly later than the crocuses, hanging out deep blue bell-shaped flowers from multiple stalks.

Glory-of-the-snow (*Chionodoxa luciliae*). A very early blooming bulb with a delicate powder-blue color fading to cream or white centers. This is among the prettiest flowers of early spring.

Puschkinia scilloides libanotica. Carries most interesting flowers of white striped with turquoise or blue-green. It blooms along with Siberian squill and glory-of-the-snow.

European pasque-flower (*Anemone pulsatilla*). Although it blooms a few weeks later than the earliest bulbs, it makes beautiful bluish purple–to–reddish purple flowers, followed later by silky, feathery leaves. It appears just before the daffodils open in most areas.

down, then cover the beds with a four inch mix of compost and soil, tamp it down and then water the bulbs.

These bulbs herald the beginning of the horticultural year. But in earliest spring, all we have are snowdrops and crocuses. And that is enough to renew our hopes and warm our hearts.

GARLAND SPIREA & WHITE SPRING BULBS

Spiraea × arguta, Tulipa 'White Parrot' *& Narcissus* hybrids

Using a Swath of White to Separate Colors

Grand white gardens of the kind made famous by Vita Sackville-West at Sissinghurst Castle in England have a refreshing, sculptural look. Whole gardens of white often look like wedding cakes, with bunting and gathers of frosting everywhere. They are as amusing as they are lovely. On the other hand, small all-white gardens, such as in a garden room that is 10 by 10 feet, give one pause. Limited color may render them stately, but the choice of white is subtractive: something is gone from this garden, like a room only just vacated.

Many gardeners prefer a garden with swatches of white—among other themes—to one that is all white. Plant choices are not determined solely by the need to keep the design entirely white all season long—through a succession of bloom. Instead, white can be used more selectively, in particular to separate areas with radically different color schemes or purposes. In the

GARLAND SPIREA & WHITE SPRING BULBS

	Zones	Height	Light	Soil	Highlights
Spiraea × arguta	4–8	4–5 ft.	Full sun.	Average well-drained soil.	Clusters of small white flowers encrust slender arching stems. in mid-spring.

Comments: *Spiraea prunifolia* 'Plena' is the bridal wreath spiraea and even more appropriate for this plant marriage.

	Zones	Height	Light	Soil	Highlights
Tulipa 'Parrot'	3–7	12–18 in.	Sun to light shade.	Rich, moist soil.	The fancy 'White Parrot' tulips have frilled petals.

Comments: Many other kinds of white tulips and favorite spring bulbs are available to lengthen the season of this plant marriage.

spring garden, a spirea surrounded by white-flowered bulbs such as 'White Parrot' tulips, 'Stainless' or 'Ice Follies' daffodils, and the white form of the snake's-head fritillary (*Fritillaria meleagris* 'Alba') makes a perfect transition between a stand of highly-colored flowers like rhododendrons and a grassy walkway or lawn.

The garland spirea (*Spiraea × arguta*) makes a showy display of its virginal flower clusters, which open in flat formations along the arching stems in May. Its aptly named cousin, bridal wreath spirea (*Spiraea prunifolia* 'Plena'), is a somewhat smaller, more delicate substitute. It blooms with thick clusters of lovely, tiny, roselike white flowers, set along slender stems. These fall out gracefully from the top of an open, vase-shaped form, creating an utterly charming effect.

It is wise to place the daffodils

between the tulips and the spirea, so the blue-green of the daffodil foliage can mediate between the yellow-green tulip leaves and the medium-green shrub. The daffodil flowers approximate the white of the spirea more closely than the white-and-green-tinged tulips. Or take this green-and-white tulip idea a step further and plant *Tulipa viridiflora* 'Spring Green', a white cottage-type flower with green flares on each petal. Most spring bulbs have white forms, and there is plenty of room for adding favorite varieties to this group, from white scilla to white hyacinths.

These bulbs will do well in humus-rich garden soil, as will the spirea. All need plenty of moisture, and all enjoy full sun. Tulips need replacing every few years, but the daffodils will take little if any work over time. Spirea looks its open, airy, floriferous best if canes over two years old are removed on a yearly basis during dormancy, as it blooms on one-year-old wood.

When its bloom is finished, spirea will melt back into invisibility in the shrub border but it will stand out again in fall when its leaves turn a bronzy, reddish orange. Even out of bloom, however, it remains an attractively shaped shrub with finely cut leaves.

White parrot tulips and the arching woody branches of garland spiraea (Spiraea × arguta), seen here covered with their spring blossoms, make a white marriage that is useful for separating different color passages.

A Gallery of White-Flowered Trees

The marriage of white spirea and spring bulbs could use the consecration of a white-flowered tree above it. Trees that bloom white at the same approximate season as the marriage include some very choice specimens. In addition to these trees, do not forget the fragrant white lilacs (*Syringa*) that would nicely accompany a spirea-bulb display:

Dogwoods (*Cornus* spp.). Choose from the pagoda dogwood (*C. alternifolia*) which is hardy to Zone 3, flowering dogwood (*C. florida*) and kousa dogwood (*C. kousa*) both hardy to Zone 5, or mountain dogwood (*C. nuttallii*), hardy to Zone 6, for beautiful white blooms from late April to May.

English hawthorn (*Crataegus laevigata*). A compact, tidy-looking tree that reaches 15 to 20 feet in Zones 4 to 9 and covers itself with clusters of small white flowers in May.

Flowering crabapples (*Malus* spp.). Big bursts of white in May are given by Japanese flowering crabapple (*M. floribunda*), tea crabapple (*M. hupehensis*), 'Red Jade' crabapple (*M.* × 'Red Jade'), and Sargent crabapple (*M. sargentii*). All are spectacular in bloom and hardy to Zone 4.

Fragrant snowbell (*Styrax obassia*). The tree reaches 20 feet or more and hangs long racemes of white fragrant flowers beneath its large leaves. Hardy to Zone 6.

Hally Joviette cherry (*Prunus* × 'Hally Joviett'). This cherry produces masses of pink buds that open to double white flowers over two or three weeks in May. Hardy to Zone 5.

Magnolias (*Magnolia* spp.). Southern magnolia (*M. grandiflora*) grows well in Zone 7 and warmer, where it produces huge white blossoms with a heady, citrusy perfume from April through August. Another species, *M.* × *loebneri* 'Merrill', is hardy to Zone 4 and produces starlike flowers.

Mountain ash (*Sorbus* spp.). The Korean mountain ash (*S. alnifolia*) and European mountain ash, also known as the Rowan tree (*S. aucuparia*), produce clusters of white flowers in May. The real show comes in September when the red berries mature. Both are hardy to Zone 3.

Ussurian pear (*Pyrus ussuriensis*). A hardy Chinese native (to Zone 4) that reaches 30 feet with pink buds that open white in May. A maintenance-free tree that needs no pruning.

Yellowwood (*Cladrastis lutea*). This full-size, native tree, hardy in Zones 5 to 8, is not planted in American gardens enough. It only blooms every few years, but when it does it really puts on a show of intensely fragrant hanging clusters of white pealike flowers. It is a June bloomer, so associate it with late white tulips, such as 'Spring Snow' or 'Shirley', and the later-blooming vanhoutte spiraea (*Spiraea* × *vanhouttei*), which are both hardy from Zone 4 to 7.

Good Background Plants

When grown as permanent plants, daffodils' foliage must be left alone to die back naturally and entirely, or they will fail to increase or to flower, and may even die out. A patch of variegated hostas at the front of the planting will help hide the bulb foliage during its less attractive, fading phase.

Hostas take shade or partial shade, which can be thrown by nearby tall perennials and the spirea later in the summer.

*Mountain dogwood (*Cornus nuttallii*), above—with its profusion of white flowers in early spring—would be a welcome addition to the spirea and bulbs. Another white passage devoted to separating areas of bright color, this marriage of irises and white stocks (*Matthiola hybrida*), opposite, blooms in midsummer.*

TULIPS, SPRUCE & JAPANESE FOREST GRASS

Tulipa batalinii 'Bronze Charm', *Picea glauca* 'Conica'
& *Hakonechloa macra* 'Aureola'

Quiet Contrasts in Form, Color, and Texture

A combination of multiple contrasting characteristics does not have to result in an assault on the senses: It is possible to combine plants that contrast in every way and yet keep the combination subtle. Of course, some plants, such as Japanese maples (*Acer palmatum*), have a delicacy and suggestiveness of form that would be demeaned by anything ostentatious or brash, such as yuccas or sunflowers, and choosing a partner requires care.

Japanese forest grass (*Hakonechloa macra* 'Aureola') is just such a delicate plant. This lovely grass gives the impression of a small bamboo, with softly-arching masses of light yellow leaves striped with green. It is easy to imagine extensive areas of it flowing over low rocks in a Japanese mountain dell. To make this discrete grass visible, pair it with plants whose forms provide strong contrast. It can be perfectly matched with the big orange-cream flowers of *Tulipa batalinii* 'Bronze Charm' and the fine, soft, short needles of the dwarf Alberta spruce, *Picea glauca* 'Conica'. Such a combination would make an excellent edging for a walkway or on a low wall.

This is a magnificent combination for the May garden. The yellow-gold of the grass is picked up and varied in the tulip flowers, and these are set off against the gray-green spruce needles. The tulip's narrow leaves are a rich, dark green, which contrasts with the other two plants as well as with the tulip flowers. The textures mix beautifully, too: the long, flowing form of the ornamental grass contrasts with the short spiky-looking needles of the spruce.

When making as serene and subtle a grouping as this, be sure to isolate it from other plants that may interfere with its quiet beauty. Stones, a garden bench, or neutral shrubs will set it off from the rest of the landscape.

TULIPS, SPRUCE & JAPANESE FOREST GRASS

	Zones	Height	Light	Soil	Highlights
Tulipa batalinii 'Bronze Charm'	4–8	10 in.	Partial shade to full sun.	Good, sandy loam.	Creamy, yellow-orange flowers open in April.

Comments: Species tulips in general tend toward rich yellow colors and can be substituted for *T. batalinii* in this association

	Zones	Height	Light	Soil	Highlights
Picea glauca 'Conica'	3–8	6–10 ft.	Partial shade to full sun.	Good, sandy loam.	Evergreen with delightful conical form and soft, gray-green needles.

Comments: Will keep interest in winter when the other partners in the group are gone.

	Zones	Height	Light	Soil	Highlights
Hakonechloa macra 'Aureola'	7–9	18 in.	Partial shade.	Good, sandy loam.	Grown for its golden yellow, arching foliage.

Comments: The all-green species is nearly as pretty and is very effective mixed with the gold-and-green cultivar.

All of these plants are fine specimens on their own, and, interestingly, all three are superb container plants. So each could be planted in its own container, then be brought together during the tulip's blooming period, and then separated when the tulips have died

The contrast of form and color among this trio of plants is strong, but not jarring. The creamsicle colors of Tulipa batalinii *'Bronze Charm' harmonize with the yellow and green grassy leaves of* Hakonechloa macra *'Aureola' and the grey-green needles of* Picea glauca *'Conica'.*

down. If planting in containers, use the tulips with *Lamium maculatum* 'Beacon Silver', so that when the tulip foliage is gone, the green and white variegated lamium will grow to fill the container and spill over its sides.

The spruce will grow in a variety of soils, but it does not like too much strong sun, hot and drying summer winds, or cold winter winds. A protected spot in the dappled shade of a larger, deciduous tree is perfect. The hakonechloa likes partial shade, too, and will tolerate the full shade of a wooded setting. Tulips like full sun

early in the year while they are blooming, and then will do fine in a partially shaded location until their leaves wither.

The right soil for these three is a good, sandy loam rich in humus. Drainage should be free and easy, but the soil should be kept moist, especially during the tulip season.

The spruce is a slow grower. After a lifetime it will hardly exceed 10 feet, and can easily be kept much smaller with occasional and judicious pruning in late winter. Do not prune it routinely, however, or it will eventually lose its charming conical shape. The *Hakonechloa* spreads slowly by underground runners and is a well-behaved plant. The tulips will return every year unless gophers or field mice get the bulbs first. If rodents are a problem, plant the bulbs in fine-mesh wire baskets sunk into the soil to ground level. This combination, once established, not only takes minimal work—it prefers to be left alone.

Other Choices

To put this combination together sucessfully in the garden, you will need to live in Zone 7 or warmer because the *Hakonechloa* will not survive in colder regions. In cold areas, substitute *Pennisetum alopecuroides* or *Briza maxima*, both grasses with an arching habit.

Besides the Japanese forest grass, other plants that might produce a similar look include the sedges, particularly the leather-leaf sedge, *Carex buchananii*—hardy to Zone 7—whose arching, 2- to 3-foot, reddish bronze leaves would blend beautifully with the tulips. Any of the golden-leaved hostas—*Hosta sieboldiana* 'Gold Edge', for example—would also work well as a substitute for the grass in colder regions.

*Two marriages, right, demonstrate combinations of strong-but-gentle contrasting forms: blue spruce (*Picea pungens*) with weigela, top; and hakonechloa with hostas, bottom. The annual greater quaking grass (*Briza maxima*), opposite, will act as a dramatic substitute for the Japanese forest grass for gardeners north of Zone 7.*

GREIGII TULIPS & RIBBON GRASS

Tulipa hybrida 'Greigii' & *Phalaris arundinacea* var. *picta*

Linear Contrasts in the Spring Garden

When you choose a classic contrast like softly curving lines with straight lines, you often get classic effects. Think of the way clematis casually drapes itself on an angular fence, for instance, or tall delphinium spires soar above rounded shrub roses. The curves of 'Greigii' hybrid tulips surrounded by a bristly grass is another example. Whenever curves meet straight lines, they set up an interesting tension, and so are good candidates for featured spots in the garden. For this classical combination, look for sites that are frequently seen, as this dramatic pairing deserves to be a focal point in the garden.

Greigii tulips are large-flowered, dwarf tulips with a lovely conical form just before full bloom, which happens late, in May into early June, depending on latitude. All the Greigii hybrids' leaves are striped or flecked with dull brownish-purple variegations. Even without their flowers, these leaves add interest to any garden. This tulip's flowers run to pink, red, orange, cream, and yellow—colors that harmonize beautifully with its own leaves.

There is something stunning about the rough ribbon grass paired with such delicate tulips. The broad, wavy-edged tulip leaves contrast well with the spiky, erect, almost prickly-looking leaves of ribbon grass, *Phalaris arundinacea* var. *picta*. Its variegations, light green and white stripes running the length of the slender blades, look superb against

*Greigii tulips undulate sensually amid the upstanding, prickly looking leaves of ribbon grass (*Phalaris arundinacea *var.* picta*).*

GREIGII TULIPS & RIBBON GRASS

	Zones	Height	Light	Soil	Highlights
Tulipa hybrida 'Greigii'	4–9	12–18 in.	Partial shade or sun.	Rich, moist, well-drained soil.	Perfect tulip-shaped flowers in reds, creams, pinks, yellows, oranges. Leaves spotted brown-purple.

Comments: Tulips need to be replaced frequently, as they typically only last a few seasons—they do not naturalize like daffodils or other spring bulbs.

	Zones	Height	Light	Soil	Highlights
Phalaris arundinacea var. *picta*	4–9	12 in.	Shade or sun.	Any type of soil suits this plant.	Light green and white striped foliage, turns buff-colored in fall.

Comments: A vigorous spreader, it may need root confinement. Substitute clump-forming grasses like *Carex* spp. and *Pennisetum* spp. if necessary.

DOWNY CLEMATIS & GOLDEN PRIVET

Clematis macropetala & *Ligustrum ovalifolium* 'Aureum'

The Metamorphosis of a Plain Hedge

Combining plants of very different habit and structure can produce some of the most interesting plant marriages. Vines and climbing perennials, for instance, can be used to decorate useful but lackluster trees and shrubs, much the way lights are strung on Christmas trees or brightly colored streamers are used to decorate bannisters. A rather plain, utilitarian hedge can be brought to life by the addition of a brightly flowered plant trained to grow through it.

A small, inconspicuous barberry or boxwood hedge, for instance, can be brightened considerably by the presence of one of the trailing campanulas. *Campanula rotundifolia*, or bluebells-of-Scotland, as it is commonly called, is

*A golden privet (*Ligustrum ovalifolium *'Aureum') is beautifully decorated by the spring-blooming downy clematis (*Clematis macropetala*).*

DOWNY CLEMATIS & GOLDEN PRIVET

	Zones	Height	Light	Soil	Highlights
Clematis macropetala	6	Vine to 10 ft.	Shade for roots, otherwise sun.	Rich, moist, acid soil.	Violet-to-blue flowers, with four large sepals and many smaller petals for flowers.

Comments: While this clematis produces smaller flowers than many, at 2 in., their form is among the most beautiful.

	Zones	Height	Light	Soil	Highlights
Ligustrum ovalifolium 'Aureum'	7	5 ft.	Full sun.	Any soil.	Grown for its gold and green semi-evergreen leaves.

Comments: Responds well to pruning. Keep it sheared to desired height with winter trimming.

easily found in catalogs. Normally it would trail languidly along the ground in front of one of these inconspicuous shrubs, but it can be coaxed to climb into the hedge's lower branches, so that it hangs bright blue bells along its wiry stems in July and August. Or one might choose the relatively rare, but gorgeous, *C. fragilis*, which opens blue and white stars at the end of its trailing 12- to 16-inch stems in late summer and fall.

Out of bloom, rhododendrons are classic background plants. They do not call attention to themselves, unless their dark masses are paired with brightly colored plants such as the tall spires of cimicifuga, ligularia, or foxtail lilies (*Eremurus* spp.).

GLOBEFLOWERS, KIRENGESHOMA & OSTRICH FERNS

Trollius europaeus, Kirengeshoma palmata & Matteuccia struthiopteris

Pairing Foliage as a Backdrop for Color

Since bright colors stand out against a dark background, it is not surprising that many gardeners place dark foliage plants behind brightly flowering ones. Nasturtium vines grown up and over a trellis in front of a mass of holly; the bright spires of loosestrife and ligularia and sage in front of a Japanese pieris (*Pieris japonica*); a drift of cerulean blue bachelor buttons in front of a Canadian hemlock (*Tsuga canadensis*)—all these stunning combinations rely on the fact that the bright colors fairly glow when seen against foliage plants that are set back into the shade.

Plants with separate, single-stalked, large flowers, rather than a mass of small blooms, look best against a dark background. Against a light background their bright points of color are easily lost. The globeflower (*Trollius europaeus*) is a prime example. It produces two-inch, very double, buttercuplike yellow globes

GLOBEFLOWERS, KIRENGESHOMA & OSTRICH FERNS

	Zones	Height	Light	Soil	Highlights
Trollius europaeus 'Aureo-variegata'	4	2 ft.	Full sun to part shade.	Rich, moist, well-drained humus-rich soil.	2–in. yellow globes held separately on long stems.
Comments: Another species, *T. ledebourii,* has more open, orange flowers.					
Kirengeshoma palmata	7	3–4 ft.	Partial shade.	Rich, moist, well-drained humus-rich soil.	Maple-shaped leaves, lovely yellow, bell-shaped flowers appear singly in fall.
Comments: Worthwhile but not easy to find. One of the flowering maples (*Abutilon* spp.) grown in pots may be substituted.					
Matteuccia struthiopteris	3	5 ft.	Partial shade.	Rich, moist, woodsy soil.	Tall and stately feathery plume-like fronds make a bold statement.
Comments: These large ferns spread by underground runners, which sprout new crowns. Its fronds die back before frost.					

on long stems and is a subtle and exquisite plant to put before a border planted toward its western side.

One might put *Kirengeshoma palmata*, a wonderful plant that grows to about two feet tall, right behind the globeflower.

*A pairing of ostrich ferns (*Matteuccia struthiopteris*) and kirengeshoma (*Kirengeshoma palmata*) creates a dark-leaved backdrop for globeflowers (*Trollius europaeus*).*

This Japanese native carries maplelike leaves and, in September and October, nodding, cup-shaped yellow flowers on the ends of arching, purplish stems.

If fairly low backdrop plants—like the kirengeshoma or azaleas—are used, they can be backed up in turn by four- to five-foot tall, stately, feathery ferns such as ostrich fern (*Matteuccia struthiopteris*) which thrives in deep shade. The effect is a deepening shadow behind the bright flowers. (Interestingly, in the north, ostrich fern also tolerates full sun.) Royal fern (*Osmunda regalis*) is similar in appearance to ostrich fern except that it grows to 6 feet tall in a stately vase shape.

Both ferns are hardy to Zone 3. The globeflower is hardy to Zone 4 and prefers a moist soil with either full sun or partial shade, although ideally it should have afternoon shade. *Kirengeshoma palmata* is hardy at least to Zone 7. All these plants like rich, moist, woodsy soil on the acid side.

Other Choices

There are many other brightly colored flowers that would show well against a dark background. The red blooms of geum, the ball-shaped flowers of the ornamental onion, the spires of cimicifuga, and delphinium, and the simple, open blossoms of Japanese anemones (*Anemone × hybrida*) in the fall are a few of many perennial choices. Among annuals, begonias, plumed thistles (*Cirsium japonicum*), and scabiosas all hold their flowers separately.

For the kirengeshoma, one could sub-

Choice Ferns to Back Up Bright Flowers

Ferns not only provide a splendid background for brightly colored flowers, they also grow to hide the spent foliage of the early bulbs. Besides the ostrich fern and royal fern, here are several other ferns that serve well in gardens all across America in Zone 3 and warmer.

Maidenhair fern (*Adiantum pedatum*) grows to 18 inches tall with feathery, light-green fronds and is a good choice to associate with bergenia and tulips.

Japanese painted fern (*Athyrium goeringianum* 'Pictum') makes a pretty display of its light green fronds that are good for massing behind plants like foam flower (*Tiarella* spp.) with its white foamy flower spikes and the diminutive *Astilbe chinensis* 'Pumila' with its raspberry-colored flower heads in early August.

Hay-scented fern (*Dennstaedtia punctilobula*) throws its fronds this way and that in shady spots, nicely backing up forward plants like *Potentilla* 'Miss Willmott' and geums.

Cinnamon fern (*Osmunda cinnamomea*) grows to 5 feet tall in a stately vase shape and makes a dramatic backdrop for bright and showy flowers like Maltese cross (*Lychnis chalcedonica*) and Oriental poppies (*Papaver orientale*).

---

stitute flowering maple (*Abutilon hybridum*), which has woody stems and grows to six or eight feet; unfortunately, it is hardy only to Zone 9. It does, however, take to pot culture and is widely grown in colder regions where it can be taken indoors in the winter.

In addition to ferns, there are many choices for background plants. Yews, Japanese black and mugo pines (*Pinus thunbergiana* and *P. mugo*), hemlocks, Norway spruces (*Picea abies*), and many other needled evergreens are traditional in the back of the border to make a backdrop for flowering shrubs. Broad-leaved evergreen hedges like privet, and plants with attractive foliage that are out of flower can all be used successfully to make a background behind bright flowers.

If the landscape lacks suitable background shrubs, plant evergreens that

like partial shade near the edges of existing trees. Rhododendrons, camellias, enkianthus, euonymus, fatsia, hydrangeas, junipers, leucothoe, skimmias and several viburnums all are good shrubs to edge the trees and provide a backdrop for color. They are especially good when planted on the east side of trees so that they are shaded from midday on. If there are no trees on the property, plant these shrubs on the western side of the garden to throw afternoon shade, and plant perennials and annuals in front of them.

*Deep, rich, fiery red and orange canna flowers smoulder in the shade created by a tropical-looking collection of feathery tree-of-heaven (*Ailanthus altissima*), huge-leaved* Gunnera mannicata, *the catalpa-like leaves of the princess tree (*Paulownia tomentosa*), and a Japanese banana (*Musa basjoo*) in a container.*

TUFTED PANSIES & ALPINE PINKS

Viola cornuta 'Aureo-variegata' & *Dianthus alpinus*

Different Colors Decorate the Same Forms

Many great plant marriages are made when a single characteristic—a common linking element—is repeated in partners. Common characteristics put contrasting characteristics in relief. A very effective and subtle way to do this is to repeat the same forms in different plants, but to vary the colors, thereby highlighting the colors of the planting. In fact, most gardeners' first marriages are probably of this type, for to plant annual "mixes" (as is commonly done) is to plant seeds of a single plant in a variety of colors.

The repeating forms can be in the shapes of the flowers, the foliage, the overall growth habit, or even the fruits. For example, the variegated tufted pansy (*Viola cornuta* 'Aureo-variegata') and the alpine pink (*Dianthus alpinus*) make a good show of similar blossoms for the garden in June and contrasting colors. Both have five-lobed flowers of about

the same one-inch width, both carry their flowers in about the same profusion on the low-growing plants, and the blossoms of both present their faces to the crowd in pretty much the same way.

But what a wonderful contrast between their colors! While the pansy has variegated foliage, the pink has variegated flowers (or bicolor flowers, as blossom variegation is

typically called). The viola's lavender is cool while the dianthus' pink background with red collars is warm; and yet the colors are not so far apart that they clash.

Alpine pinks resemble the more familiar

The reversal of color displays in the similarly shaped pansies and pinks, opposite, provides a subtle contrast of opposites.

TUFTED PANSIES & ALPINE PINKS

	Zones	Height	Light	Soil	Highlights
Viola cornuta 'Aureo-variegata'	5	8 in.	Partial shade.	Average, well-drained soil.	Single, five-petalled, lavender pansies each 1 in. across.

Comments: Tufted pansies come in delicious colors, like 'Chantreyland' in apricot, plus others in ruby-red, blue, yellow, and white.

	Zones	Height	Light	Soil	Highlights
Dianthus alpinus	4	6–8 in.	Full sun to part shade.	Average, slightly alkaline soil.	Single, five-lobed, fringed, 1-in., flat-faced flowers have dark rings around their throats

Comments: The familiar cottage pinks, *D. plumarius*, are similar in appearance and can be substituted for this rather rare alpine species.

PORTUGAL LAUREL & ROSE AND WHITE CAMPION

Prunus lusitanica & *Lychnis coronaria*

Stunning Color for a Difficult Area

There are a few colors so strong that they threaten to overpower any other hue in sight. Orange and magenta come to mind: These bullies of the spectrum scream for attention, especially when combined with less assertive pastels. But used in moderation and buffered with plenty of gray or white, not only do they can become much more tractable, they can brighten up difficult areas in the garden.

Rose campion (*Lychnis coronaria*) has perhaps the most intense hue of any garden flower—an eye-popping, vibrant magenta also found in silenes and blood-red cranesbill (*Geranium sanguineum*). Its potency can make it hard to coordinate with other colors. Used in combination with whites and silvers, however, magenta works quite well and gives a very dramatic punch to an otherwise drab scene. In controlled masses this color is good, but it quickly begins to overwhelm any area if used too enthusiastically.

Plant a drift of magenta flowers amid a sweep of white ones, and use this combination to set off another plant that carries white flowers. A spectacular example

of this is the combination of rose campion with its white form (*L. coronaria* 'Alba') against a Portugal laurel (*Prunus lusitanica*). Visually, the densely branched laurel gives the impression of a waterfall of white florets, foaming as they reach the bottom and flowing away on a white and magenta tide. The campions' silvery leaves and stems branch regularly, giving a criss-cross appearance. The laurel's five- to ten-inch white flower spikes emerge from the glossy, rich green leaves and toss themselves this way and that, echoing

the criss-cross effect of the campions but also bringing a bit more order to this rather riotous, cheerful scene.

This combination blooms together in June. The laurel's spikes set fruit which will turn bright red to dark purple in July and August. The campions continue their impressive bloom through July, then fade away. At that point their silvery gray foliage continues to grace the scene until late summer, when it too fades away. By fall, the laurel will stand alone—unless the campions are interplanted with late-

---

PORTUGAL LAUREL & ROSE AND WHITE CAMPION

	Zones	Height	Light	Soil	Highlights
Prunus lusitanica	7-9	20 ft.	Full sun.	Average-to-poor, well-drained soil.	Small tree or shrub, lustrous evergreen leaves, spikes of fragrant white flowers in spring. Tolerates drought.

Comments: Use cold-hardy *Prunus virginiana* or *P. maackii* in northerly regions. Grows many stems or can be pruned to a single trunk.

	Zones	Height	Light	Soil	Highlights
Lychnis coronaria	3–8	2–3 ft.	Full sun.	Average-to-poor garden soil.	Intense magenta flowers on striking gray-green silvery leaved stems.

Comments: The white form, 'Alba', mixed with the intense magenta helps to alleviate the eye-popping color.

blooming flowers, such as asters. (These begin blooming in late August and will provide color almost to frost.) The tree's leaves will finish the season with a bright display of autumn color.

While the laurel and the campions

The vibrant magenta of rose campion (Lychnis coronaria) is so strong that white is the best choice for an association; here it is grouped with the white form (L. coronaria 'Alba') and the tossing flower spikes of Portugal laurel (Prunus lusitanica).

will grow beautifully in good soil, they are tolerant of a wide variety of soil conditions. The laurel is also tolerant of summer droughts, such as those experienced in many western states.

Portugal laurel grows to be a small tree, to about ten to twenty feet tall after many years. To look best with the two- to three-foot campion, allow the laurel to grow as a multi-trunked shrub, rather than pruning it to a single-trunked tree. This way, its many limbs will hang nearly to the ground and merge with the campion flowers.

Other Choices

The campions are related to the Maltese-cross (*Lychnis chalcedonica*) and German catchfly (*L. viscaria*), favorites in perennial gardens in Europe and America. They can be sown as annuals, as well, but both 'Purpurea' and 'Alba' are hardy in all parts of the country and will perform as reliable perennials, reseeding themselves like weeds in good soil. It is easy to hoe out excess plants when they are emerging in spring.

Portugal laurel is hardy only to about

WILLOW-LEAVED PEAR & COLLARETTE DAHLIAS

Pyrus salicifolia 'Pendula' & *Dahlia* 'Bishop of Llandaff'

A Study in Habits

Plants can assume an almost infinite range of postures: prostrate, weeping, rounded, open, upright, fastigiate. One of their most overt characteristics, posture is generally not given much thought—good gardeners, when planning a garden, consider posture almost automatically. But elevating the status of this characteristic, until it is a basis for selecting marriage mates, can produce startling and beautiful pairings.

What, for instance, would look best with an upright posture to make a pleasing combination? Lombardy poplars (*Populus nigra* 'Italica'), for example, have an extremely erect posture, a form horticulturists call "fastigiate." These trees hold themselves bolt upright and lift their arms close to the trunk, producing a tower effect.

To answer this question, consider combinations of forms that you find beautiful. Do not limit yourself to gardening conventions. I have always found the form of suspension bridges, for instance, with their sweeping horizontal spans supported by towers at each end, to be particularly graceful.

WILLOW-LEAVED PEAR & COLLARETTE DAHLIAS					
	Zones	Height	Light	Soil	Highlights
Pyrus salicifolia 'Pendula'	5–9	25 ft.	Full sun.	Average garden soil.	Silver foliage on a graceful weeping form.
Comments: Like most pears, this variety is susceptible to fire blight. If this is a problem in your area, try to find resistant varieties or substitute Russian olive (*Elaegnus angustifolia*). If a problem arises with fire blight, immediately prune out affected branches and burn them.					
Dahlia 'Bishop of Llandaff'	10	2–3 ft.	Full sun.	Rich, moist, soil.	Large "collarette" flowers of intense scarlet.
Comments: Avoid using nitrogen-rich fertilizer on dahlias, as it will force weak growth and fewer flowers while contributing to mold problems during subsequent winter storage.					

Transferring this combination of forms to the garden might lead to a combination of fastigiate trees, such as the Lombardy poplar, with horizontal hedges or gracefully arching plants, wider than they are tall.

A rounded shape may be combined with several other rounded shapes of different sizes and foliage colors to make a lyrical group. A tall pyramidal form such as Chinese juniper (*Juniperus chinensis* 'Pyramidalis'), a white spruce (*Picea glauca* 'Conica'), or a dawn red-wood (*Metasequoia glyptostroboides*) would make a fine contrast with a deciduous tree with sinuous, spreading limbs like a sargent crabapple (*Malus sargentii*).

Marriages of postures can be any size as long as each partner is in proportion to its neighbor. Even container plants can be combined for their habits. A remarkable duo is made, for instance, by a container of spotted lamium (*Lamium maculatum* 'Beacon Silver')

A Sense of Proportion:
The Golden Section

Proportion is, of course, essential to any composition, including plant marriages, but because it comes as second nature, generally it does not warrant discussion. Proportion determines the size of elements that make up any composition and their placement in relation to one another. It is worth mentioning, though, when one is pairing forms or, in this case, postures, where it is particularly vital. One would not, for instance, marry groundcovers with redwoods: any sense of combination would be lost to the vast difference in scale.

There is a school of thought, dating back to the Ancient Greeks, that believes the ideal, or most pleasing, place to break a horizontal line is at 8/13 of the way from one end. At this point the horizontal line is broken in such a way that the smaller section is in the same proportion to the larger section as the larger section is to the whole.

This "ideal" proportion can also be used to determine the appropriate sizes of the partners. A pleasant size contrast occurs when one form is roughly 8/13ths the size of the larger one. If this rule is to be applied to plant forms, the measurements should reflect the plants' sizes at maturity. Pairings made to this proportion will strike a pleasing balance of size. Of course, such a guide should not be followed scrupulously, but it may prove helpful when planning combinations.

*The gentle, upright form of dark-leaved red dahlias (*Dahlia *'Bishop of Llandaff') reaches up to meet the twisting, tumbling form of the willow-leaved pear (*Pyrus salicifolia *'Pendula'), with its bright silvery leaves. The result is a superb marriage of unlikely partners of opposite postures.*

Handling Gladiolus in the Garden

Gladiolus blooms from 65 to 100 days after its corms are planted in good, moist soil. A scape—its flower stalk—will bloom for about a week and a half. So, for a long bloom season over the summer, stagger plantings from March or April through June, which will give bloom from June through September.

Plant the corms about three to four times deeper than their height and from four to six inches apart in all directions, depending on their size.

Depending on growth rate and personal sense of aesthetics, some staking of the flower stalks may be needed. Insert slender green sticks, available at garden centers, near the base of the plant and attach the flower stalk from behind with similarly colored twist ties, lightly applied. If stalks appear able to stand by themselves, let them.

When the foliage yellows and starts to die back, dig out the corms—you will find the original ones and some new ones—and cut off the leaves 2 inches above the corm. Dry these in a shaded place for several weeks, then pull off the old original corms and store the younger ones (from 1½ to 2 inches across, no larger) in a cool, dry place where they will not rot. You can dust them with Bordeaux mixture to prevent mold or rot from growing during storage. The best corms will be high-crowned young ones less than a couple of inches across.

fact, of the blossoms of a certain species of cranesbill (*Geranium pratense*) scattered around it. In addition, there are cranesbills, such as *G. argenteum* and *G. cinereum*, with petals thinly veined in a red that echoes the red of the gladiolus flowers. Overcast light and raindrops only intensify the colors of these two plants. The soft pink buds and creamy white flowers of *Astrantia major* soften the marriage by adding an elegant, lacy touch.

The intense and unusual color of *Gladiolus byzantinus* 'Ruber' makes it a very choice member of the gladiolus clan. Gladiolus are so visually strong that they are hard to coordinate with other flowers in the garden. Consequently many gardeners grow them only as cut flowers, if they grow them at all. But *G. byzantinus* 'Ruber' has a color around which an excellent plant marriage can be built. They are also quite attractive even when out of bloom; each corm sends up five sword-shaped leaves, which add smooth, clean lines that will distract attention from less striking plants, such as the astrantia and geranium's rather unattractive,

*Warm color harmonies can be created in several different palettes. Such flowering favorites as shrubby Spanish lavender (*Lavandula stoechas var. *pedunculata), opposite, which gives a long season of bloom, is married with* Dianthus *'Lilian', for a pretty combination of pinks and purples. The long-blooming pink brushes of* Polygonum bistorta, *are married with* Iris Sibirica *and ranunculus for another marriage of pink and purple color harmonies, highlighted by a white accent, above right.*

scratchy-looking leaves. The cranesbill, however, is useful because its season of bloom is so long, from late spring to killing frost.

Astrantias, which are perennials frequently seen in English gardens, are used far too seldom in America. They are European natives from Spain to the Black Forest, then all the way east to Russia and south to Bulgaria, and have globular flower heads that feature bracts, which resemble lace collars. Their foliage melts into the background of this association, as it closely resembles that of cranesbills. The variety 'Rosensymphonie' is deep rose-pink, while 'Rubra' is dark, rich red.

All members of this association like full sun, good garden soil, and adequate water over summer, although the astrantia and gladiolus can take some drought. The gladiolus flowers for about ten days. By making successive plantings, you can have bloom from June into August. (See the box, opposite, for planting tips to extend the gladiolus' flowering season.) Cranesbills are known for their naturally long periods of bloom, and this species is no exception; it is in full flower from June to August with scattered blossoms until frost. Astrantias are also long-bloomers, flowering from June to September.

Other Choices

This particular gladiolus can be hard to find in some parts of the country. Instead you could substitute one of the more widely available hybrids, garden gladiolus (*Gladiolus* x *hortulanus*), with strong color. Few other flowers, however, can match the bluish red intensity of *Gladiolus byzantinus* 'Ruber'.

Another species of cranesbill, *Geranium himalayense*, has lilac petals with purple veins and a red-purple eye; it blooms all summer, and would be as at home in this association as *G. pratense* because of its reddish colors.

The astrantia is hardy to Zone 7 or 8, depending on the spot, so it can be used in southern and Sun Belt gardens. Further north, feverfew cultivars, such as *Chrysanthemum parthenium* 'Silver Ball' for instance, would make an appropriate replacement, as would the white and pink types of globe amaranth (*Gomphrena globosa*). Both of these plants have even longer seasons of bloom than astrantias. Globe amaranth flowers have the added attraction of drying as everlastings on the plant, so that they can easily be brought into the house for winter arrangements.

BOX HONEYSUCKLE & PURPLE SMOKE TREE

Lonicera nitida 'Baggesen's Gold' & *Cotinus coggygria* 'Purpureus'

The Drama of Unusual Foliage Colors

While there are seemingly countless different foliage colors, many gardens still end up being largely, masses of green. Flowers are useful in providing color contrast, but they tend to be short-lived. For the rest of the growing season, plants with foliage colors other than green offer long-term interest and can help distinguish a garden from a yard.

Plant marriages of contrasting foliage can have tremendous dramatic impact; an explosion of purple, with a golden halo hovering around it, for instance, makes an indelible mark in the landscape. When thrown together, something very interesting happens to bright gold and muted, dark purple: The gold stands out and appears to reach forward, while the purple, which absorbs light, recedes. The result is a contrast of light and dark, of value rather than hue.

The combination of purple smoke tree and golden box honeysuckle, which represents this contrast, is a wonderful, exotic antidote to a too-green landscape. The purple smoke tree, a hardy decidu-

ous shrub, produces big puffs of purplish-lavender "smoke" at the branch tips as the flower stalks elongate in summer. Covered with fine, filamentous hairs, these flowers give it a wispy appearance. The leaves of the golden box honeysuckle create a tight frenzy of gilt droplets. As a backdrop to the stately smoke tree, it is stunning. When the smoke tree is in bloom, the association with the box honeysuckle is even more dramatic, because the wispy flowers and busy honeysuckle leaves make a beauti-

ful marriage of form and color.

A second smoke tree, planted carefully at the back of the border, echoes the gold and purple association. This kind of repetition of color or form helps pull the garden together and unifies it

Plant marriages based on interesting shrub foliage color are among the most exciting combinations for the garden. The striking bronze foliage of the box honeysuckle makes a dramatic backdrop to the dark purple leaves of the smoke tree.

BOX HONEYSUCKLE & PURPLE SMOKE TREE

	Zones	Height	Light	Soil	Highlights
Lonicera nitida 'Baggesen's Gold'	7–9	6–8 ft.	Full sun.	Average soil.	Striking gold, evergreen leaves, white flowers in June.

Comments: Tiny leaves, which resemble boxwood, are evergreen, turning bronze to plum color in winter. Tends to be unruly, needs pruning.

	Zones	Height	Light	Soil	Highlights
Cotinus coggygria 'Purpureus'	5–9	20 ft.	Full sun.	Average soil.	Spring leaves are purple, fading to green; impressive pink-lavender flower puffs appear in July.

Comments: The cultivar 'Royal Purple' holds its purple leaf color throughout the summer, as opposed to 'Purpureus', which slowly fades to green over time.

EUROPEAN WHITE BIRCH & WHITE SIEBOLD'S HOSTA

Betula pendula & *Hosta sieboldiana* 'Elegans'

An Elegant Combination of Foliage and Bark

Flowers are fleeting. They are here and then gone, sometimes within days; rarely do they last more than a few weeks. To create a more lasting addition to the landscape, one that will remain interesting for a long season, you cannot do better than to design a plant marriage based on the combination of interesting bark, such as *Pinus bungeana*, Japanese stewartia (*Stewartia pseudocamellia*), or white birch (*Betula papyrifera*), and long-lasting foliage of evergreens and perennials like ferns.

European white birch (*Betula pendula*) and white Siebold's hosta (*Hosta sieboldiana* 'Elegans') make a lovely marriage that keeps improving itself for much of the growing season. This is a restful association for the yard, as might be seen from the patio. In the spring, the hosta pierces the soil and unfurls its big leaves to cover the fading foliage of the earliest spring bulbs. The birch's white bark contrasts beautifully with the hosta's rich, dark, blue-green leaves. As June progresses, the hosta leaves reach their full

	Zones	Height	Light	Soil	Highlights
BETULA PENDULA & HOSTA SIEBOLDIANA 'ELEGANS'					
Betula pendula	2–6	30–40 ft.	Full sun.	Prefers a moist, humus-rich soil.	Gleaming white, papery, peeling bark. On older trees, branches droop gracefully.
Comments: Where bronze birch borers are a problem, substitute *Betula platyphylla japonica*, a resistant white-barked species.					
Hosta sieboldiana 'Elegans'	3–8	2–3 ft.	Shade.	Rich, moist, humus-rich soil.	Large blue-green leaves with a corduroy texture, white flowers in July and August.
Comments: The cultivar 'Frances Willliams' has golden leaf margins, and would associate well with the fall leaf color of birch trees.					

size, up to a foot across, and acquire a dusty patina.

By late July, the hostas' flower scapes appear and hang out their white lilylike blossoms. Now the white of the birch bark is repeated in the pristine white hosta blossoms. To reproduce this effect, be sure to get the cultivar 'Elegans', for others of this species—and most other hosta varieties as well—have lavender flowers. An exception is *Hosta plantaginea* with its white blossoms and heady

fragrance. Unfortunately, the leaves of this species are rather coarse compared to those of 'Elegans' and so it cannot compare in this combination. But, as luck would have it, 'Elegans' is hardy and will thrive almost everywhere there is sufficient shade.

The clean look of the white birch bark is a refined partner for the dark blue-green color and seersucker texture of the leaves of Hosta sieboldiana *'Elegans'.*

Good Background Plants

A planting of lady ferns (*Athyrium filix-femina*) would further dress up this association. These hardy, deciduous ferns tolerate a wide range of soil and light conditions, and are native to the United States. The tree, hostas, and ferns provide a shady oasis in an otherwise sunny July garden.

Other Choices

Besides the European white birch, other birch species would be lovely in this kind of setting. The Japanese white

The big leaves of Hosta sieboldiana *marry well with the narrow regular leaves and yellow-green flowers of* Euphorbia characias *var.* wulfenii, *one of the evergreen spurges, opposite.* Betula jacquemontii *'Trade Clone'—a birch native to northern India and hardy to Zone 7—carries very bright white bark, above.*

birch (*Betula platyphylla japonica*) also has white bark. The river birch (*Betula nigra*) has shaggy, exfoliating bark of a soft buff color. Bark of the paper or canoe birch (*B. papyrifera*) is a range of pinkish creams. The yellow birch (*B. alleghentensi*) has curling strips of yellowish bark. The blackish, lenticulated bark of the cherry birch (*B. lenta*) is strongly aromatic. All these plants are hardy to Zone 5; the Japanese white birch is a good choice for Zones 9-11.

Both birches and hostas like plenty of water, and both prefer a rich, woodsy, humus-rich soil with good drainage—although the hostas demand it, while the birches are more tolerant of average soils.

Bronze birch borers can be an intractable problem on European white birch in the southern parts of the country, especially those where summers are very hot. Check with your local county

agricultural extension agent to see if birch borer is a problem in your area. If it is, plant a resistant birch, such as the Japanese white birch or the river birch.

Birches are also host to several species of aphids, which, if left unchecked, will spot hosta leaves with droplets that encourages sooty molds which can discolor the hostas. If any aphids are seen, hose off the birch leaves with a strong spray of water. Encourage aphid-eating beneficial insects by planting a few umbelliferous plants like dill, or yarrow. These plants with umbrellalike flower heads are hosts for insects that feed on aphids.

Spring Bulbs with Hostas and Ferns

Shower the ground under birches with spring bulbs for early color. The hostas and ferns will grow up through the bulb foliage toward the end of the bulbs' flowering season, then open to cover them just as they are starting to look tired and spent.

The early spring bulbs—sanguinaria, pasque flowers (*Anemone pulsatilla*), winter aconites (*Eranthis hyemalis*), chionodoxa, scilla, puschkinia, daffodils, crocus, snowdrops , and muscari, will all provide bold splashes of color in March and April, then disappear as the subdued blue-green and white theme of the hostas and birch takes over. All these are low-growing bulbs (except the tuberous-root bloodroot) that are hardy to Zone 4.

When winter comes and all the herbaceous plants are cut back to the ground, the birch will stand alone in the garden, a reminder to the gardener of the colorful glories to come in earliest spring.

SEA HOLLY &
BELLFLOWERS

Eryngium maritimum & Campanula latifolia

Opposites Attract

The theme of opposites first clashing, then attracting, is ancient and universal, and as useful in the well-designed perennial border as in any of the other arts. When two partners in a plant marriage are truly opposite, every characteristic—color, form, texture, posture, to name a few— is in contrast. Such combinations are so striking that at first they create awesome clashes. The first impression they impart is usually one of sublime gaudiness—a stunning mismatch. These loud, attention-grabbing groupings seem to call only for instant divorce.

But this impression, however strong it may be at first, is fleeting, and once we become accustomed to seeing them together, we begin to notice just how beautiful and attractive they are. A

*Silver, spiky sea holly (*Eryngium maritimum*) and cascades of the soft bells of* Campanula latifolia *prove that opposites attract, as they shine in this excellent marriage.*

SEA HOLLY & BELLFLOWERS

	Zones	Height	Light	Soil	Highlights
Eryngium maritimum	4–8	8–10 ft.	Full sun.	Well-drained, sandy soil.	Upright branched plants; flowers have prominent cone-shaped centers with white, spiky collars.

Comments: Several species of *Eryngium*, notably *E. amethystinum* and *E. × zabelii*, have steel-blue petals and flowers that may add a new dimension to pairings with bellflowers.

	Zones	Height	Light	Soil	Highlights
Campanula latifolia	4–8	3 ft.	Partial shade.	Moist garden loam.	Showy blue to violet bells or stars that open on a center spire.

Comments: One of the neatest and most tidy of the campanulas. There is a white variety, 'Alba', that is attractive when mixed with the violet species.

prickly thistle or artichoke (*Cynara scolymus*) with *Artemisia schmidtiana* 'Silver Mound', for instance, or a sweet pea vine (*Lathyrus odoratus*) dripping clusters of rose-to-violet pea-like flowers among the upright stalks and big, rosy flowers of hollyhocks (*Alcea rosea*) might create such an impression. Plant marriages of opposites of this size will make a strong impression anywhere they can

be seen without obstruction. While their size makes them inappropriate for a centerpiece of a large-scale island bed, they will inspire strong reactions along the border of such a bed or at the heart of a smaller one. And, first impressions being what they are, it might perhaps be best to refrain from placing such marriages by the front door.

A crowd of dancing violet bellflowers

last for weeks, softening into rose-pink, as shown, then continuing to change color through September, becoming darker, redder, and more bronze—almost a rich mahogany. They finally turn dark bronze as they dry in the early frosts.

Lavender cotton has been cultivated for centuries; it was favored in knot gardens, where its gray leaves made a dramatic contrast to green hedges. Growing to two feet tall, this shrubby perennial looks cool even in the brightest sun, because of its grayness. Although it produces yellow flowers at the end of the summer, I usually trim them off, for my interest is in the foliage.

Several other gray-leaved plants, such as *artemisia* spp. and lamb's ears (*Stachys byzantina)* will give the whitish silver-to-silver gray appearance that is needed to pair with the sedum. Among the best alternatives for warmer zones are dusty miller (*Senecio cineraria*) and, in the colder regions, *Artemisia stellerana, Artemisia* 'Canescens', or silver king artemisia (*Artemisia ludoviciana* var. *albula*).

Good Background Plants

This pink and gray combination benefits from a backdrop that sets it apart in the garden. The association will benefit from an interesting setting, with creamy green-flowered plants forming a tangled backdrop. The green flowerballs of thoroughwax, a long-stemmed subshrub, for instance, might join the pendulous flowers of the evergreen hollyleaf sweetspire, whose florets scent the August air.

In areas colder than Zone 7, where sweetspire will not grow, substitute the white or pink flower spires of summersweet (*Clethra alnifolia*), another small tree. Its flowers are erect and do not have the grace of the drooping sweetspire, but they will still make a superb marriage in late summer with the sedum below. Thoroughwax is also a Zone 7 plant; in areas colder than that, you can substitute the pretty woodbine (*Lonicera periclymenum*), which produces yellow and purple flowers in summer and fall.

Sweetspire and thoroughwax like rich, moist soil, while both the sedum and lavender cotton can take drought and poorer, sandier soil. They will both thrive in the rich, well-watered soil that sustains the supporting cast, though it may make them a little more leggy than they should be.

Notice that the taller plants—the sweetspire and thoroughwax—are trained against a wall. This provides a valuable dark background for the shrubs, which themselves are background for the lighter colors of the featured marriage. But, finally, it is the sedum and lavender cotton, which need full sun, that should be positioned where they invite close inspection and can serve as the focal point of the overall design.

Handling the Unruly
Santolina

Lavender cotton *(Santolina chamaecyparissus)*, a native of the Mediterranean, can serve a multitude of purposes in the garden with its glorious gray foliage. It has a tendency, however, to be quite woody and will pose problems if not tended conscientiously.

Lavender cotton is prone to becoming leggy—growth remains lush at the top of the plant but becomes weedy below—so it needs regular pruning to keep it thick and bushy. In the fall, when the plant has flowered, cut the woody stems back to within a couple inches of the crown.

Then in the spring, when the plant is still dormant, use a shovel to cut through the root system and remove the older, woodier half. This can be replanted elsewhere or composted.

With a trowel, dig up the soil a few inches deep around the remaining plant and give it a handful of compost and a light mulching of dried leaves or grass clippings. Water it thoroughly and it will resprout and renew itself in a full, attractive shape.

*The long season and changing palette of its flowers makes sedum a garden favorite; here it has cleverly been combined with the equally long-blooming annual tree mallow (*Lavatera trimestris *'Silver Cup'), opposite. Pink and gray is a very reliable combination in the garden. A pairing of mallows and artemisia, right, provides a new approach to this winning color scheme for gardens north of Zone 6.*

COTONEASTER & SNEEZEWEED

Cotoneaster bullatus & Helenium autumnale

Ornamental Berries and Seedpods Brighten the Fall

In the late fall, when the garden floral display is reduced to chrysanthemums and a few other late-blooming composite flowers, the ripening fruits of berry- and seed-producing plants come to the rescue. Berries and seedpods most often mature in shades of red and gold, but sometimes to purple and blue-purple, like the clustered fruits of thorny greenbriers, (*Smilax herbacea* and *S. rotundifolia).*

The various berry colors afford the gardener interesting material for marriages. Certain *Cotoneaster* species are especially good for this purpose. For instance, the cotoneaster's red berries look beautiful hanging among a stand of *Helenium autumnale,* known as common sneezeweed. *H. autum-*

COTONEASTER & SNEEZEWEED

	Zones	Height	Light	Soil	Highlights
Cotoneaster bullatus	6	10–15 ft.	Full sun.	Rich, well-drained soil.	Pink flowers give way to red berries, the chief interest of this shrub.

Comments: Similar, and easier to find in nurseries, is *Cotoneaster salicifolius,* which has many choice cultivars.

	Zones	Height	Light	Soil	Highlights
Helemium autumnale	3	3 ft.	Full sun.	Rich, moist soil.	2-in. daisies bloom profusely on branching stems through the fall.

Comments: Helemium has many lovely cultivars, including 'Bruno' in red mahogany; 'Crimson beauty' in bronzy red, and 'Riverton Beauty' in yellow with maroon centers.

nale is a native American, hardy to Zone 3. It blooms into late October with yellow daisies streaked with red or reddish brown in many varieties and with yellow to reddish-brown raised centers.

Many cotoneasters are deciduous, holding showy red fruits on their bare branches into the winter. Creeping cotoneaster (*C. adpressus*) is one such deciduous species with good fruit display, an even fuller dis-

play is given by rock cotoneaster (*C. horizontalis*) Both of these hug the ground.

One of the best choices for fall color is the bearberry cotoneaster (*Cotoneaster dammeri*), an evergreen sort that is hardy to Zone 3. It hugs the ground as it makes a thick creeping mat, and carries lots of showy, one-half-inch diameter brilliant red fruit in fall. Bushy, taller species with long-lasting fruit include *C. bullatus*, a very beautiful shrub that usually grows to about ten feet tall and is hardy to Zone 6, and *C. henryanus*, which grows from ten to twelve feet tall and is hardy to Zone 7. These are semi-evergreen, or deciduous only for a short time in the dead of winter, after the association with flowering plants is well over.

The willowleaf cotoneaster (*C. salicifolius*) is one of the most beautiful of the shrubby types. It is an evergreen cotoneaster, or semi-evergreen in the coldest part of its range, where winter minimums drop below 10°F. It flowers in July and its bright crimson fruits color up in November, then hang on into the winter. It is a vigorous grower and can even be invasive in good, moist soil, reaching twelve to fifteen feet in five to eight years, with an equal or wider spread. That vigorous habit, combined with its evergreen characteristic, makes it a good screen or hedge for planting in the back of the border where it can provide a dark background for summer flowers and then bloom from November.

The garden in fall need not depend solely on the bright colors of turning foliage for excitement. There are quite a few bright gems that can be brought out to enliven the landscape. A number of seedpods and colorful fruits, such as the shiny red berries of Cotoneaster bullatus *'Firebird', burst into bright colors in the fall, and make dramatic partners for fall flowers like* Helenium autumnale, *above left.*

The marriage can be handled in one of two ways: The sneezeweed or chrysanthemum can be planted to grow up just in front of or around the ever-

*Pearly everlasting (*Anaphalis cinnamomea*), opposite, is at its peak when the rest of the garden looks poorly. When the first frosts arrive, its small pearls unfold into sumptuous white seedheads. Another interesting combination of fruit, two crabapples (*Malus 'Red Sentinel' and M. 'Butterball') display their splendid red and yellow apples, above, which will continue to hang together for a very decorative early winter.*

green cotoneaster shrub; or, drifts of the flowering perennials can be placed among the low-growing, ground-hugging forms of cotoneaster.

The berry plants and the perennials prefer full sun and rich, well-drained garden soil, although the woody cotoneasters will tolerate poor soil and dry conditions much better than the herbaceous perennials. The chrysanthemums will need division every year in early spring before growth starts to look their best. Lift and divide sneezeweed every other year to keep it from dying out. Replant with the cotoneaster to expand the bed.

Other Choices

Besides cotoneasters, similar berried shrubs include pyracanthas, hardy to Zone 7, and toyon (*Heteromeles arbutifolia*), to Zone 8. Both these bright-berried plants do very well in California. And of course there are the numerous and varied hollies, both evergreen and deciduous. Evergreen hollies are hardy to Zone 7 or 6; deciduous ones to Zone 4 or 3. Many of the traditional yellow-ochre-red-brown chrysanthemums of fall harmonize their colors with red or yellow berries and can be substituted for sneezeweed.

zontally, with the needles pointing upward from the arching fingers of the branch tips. It is here on the new wood of the tips that the silvery, blue-gray color is clustered; older wood carries needles that mature into a blue-green.

Other Choices

The spindle tree is a native of Korea and Japan, but is widely grown in the United States. Many other plants can give autumn leaf color of the same type, but few will be as brilliant as this close relative of the often-planted winged euonymus (*E. alata*), with its bright rose-red foliage in fall. If it is hard to find, substitute the more common European spindle tree (*E. europaea*). It has the same habits and shape, and turns a beautiful rose-pink in fall that looks every bit as good with the blue-green fir as *E. oxyphyllis*.

Brilliant yellow or scarlet would also be an excellent choice to associate with the red fir or blue spruce. Both such colors are given by various cultivars of smooth sumac (*Rhus glabra*) or staghorn sumac. In fact, no plant produces more intense scarlets than the sumac, and the fall leaf colors often vary into the golds, plums and burgundies.

Sumac berry clusters are showy, too. The posture of the plant is open and airy, which contrasts well with the denseness of the conifers. In winter, the sumac's long, tan, bare stems look good softly forking through the conifers.

The red fir is a native of the coast

range from southern Oregon to the San Francisco Bay, and down the spine of the Sierra Nevada mountains. It grows at elevations above 1,000 feet and may be hard to establish at sea level, in which case you could substitute the lovely Colorado blue spruce (*Picea pungens* 'Hoopsii') or the more compact 'Moerheimii' variety.

Red fir, blue spruce, and the deciduous spindle tree or European spindle tree are all hardy to Zone 5. They take full sun to partial shade and average soil conditions, though good drainage is a must. None needs excess water. Ordinary, well-drained field conditions will be fine for this association.

*Thuja occidentalis 'Rheingold', above, offers yellow-gold evergreen foliage for a fall association. Winged euonymous (*E. alata*), in its rose-red fall color, right, would partner well with 'Rheingold'.*

Other Choices for Flaming Fall Foliage

Several trees and shrubs can be substituted for the spindle tree, with similar if slightly different foliage color effects:

Dogwoods (*Cornus* spp.). Known and cherished for their fall colors, which range from yellows through oranges, reds, to purples. Most are hardy to Zone 4.

Fothergilla major. A small shrub with orange to purplish-red leaves in fall. Planted primarily for its intense and beautiful fall color. Zone 5.

Franklin tree (*Franklinia alatamaha*). A neat, compact form with rich fall color offset by waxy white flowers during fall foliage time. Spectacular with blue spruce. Zone 5.

Japanese Barberry (*Berberis thunbergii*). A shrub with leaves that turn a solid red in fall. Zone 5.

Laceleaf Japanese maple (*Acer palmatum* 'Dissectum Atropurpureum'). A prime example of a boldly colored red-foliaged plants of excellent posture. Maples in general, but especially the Japanese types, greet the fall with sheets of flame. Zone 5.

Sassafras (*Sassafras albidum*). A weed where it naturalizes, but a well-behaved small tree elsewhere. It produces a rich brocade of fall colors from purples through yellows. Zone 6.

Serviceberry (*Amelanchier laevis*). A small tree with edible berries and yellow, orange and red fall color. Zone 4.

Sumacs (*Rhus* spp.). This genus includes yellow-to-scarlet types of the smooth sumac (*R. glabra*) and the staghorn sumac (*R. typhina*). Extremely intense colors occur in *R. typhina*. Zone 5.

YELLOWTWIG AND SIBERIAN DOGWOODS & AMERICAN ARBORVITAE

Cornus stolonifera 'Flaviramea', *Cornus alba* 'Sibirica' & *Thuja occidentalis* 'Ellwangeriana Aurea'

Smoldering Fires in the Winter Landscape

All along the road the reddish, purplish, forked, upstanding, twiggy stuff of brushes and small trees...

William Carlos Williams
"Poem"

Bursting with color, exuberant of form, a well-planned winter garden exemplifies the best of what is available to the gardener in the off season.

Making the most of interesting forms, colorful barks, persistent fruits and unusual evergreen foliage color, it is possible to create an exciting and beautifully colorful landscape when all the surrounding environs are bleak reminders of the seasons just passed.

Before we delve into the beauties of the more colorful plants in the marriage of dogwoods and arborvitae, note the path and the rich green juniper in the background. It is still winter and the grass has become green. The path and juniper are integral to the beauty of this scene, for their greens provide a foil for the yellow, red, and bronze foliage in the landscaping. In areas where the grass stays green through the winter, this scene would be stable through most of the season.

The "forked, upstanding, twiggy" branches of yellowtwig dogwood (*Cornus stolonifera* 'Flaviramea') hail the viewer with its cheerful and welcoming splash of lemony yellow. In summer this is an inconspicuous, suckering, thicket-forming shrub with dirty yellow flowers, but in winter the bark becomes an inimitable focus.

In the background loom several American arborvitae (*Thuja occidentalis* 'Ellwangeriana Aurea'), whose summer-

The bright red and yellow bark of the shrubby dogwoods, placed behind the yellow-bronze arborvitae, brighten the winter landscape.

SIBERIAN DOGWOODS & AMERICAN ARBORVITAE

	Zones	Height	Light	Soil	Highlights
Cornus stolonifera 'Flaviramea'	2–8	6–8 ft.	Full sun, to part shade.	Moist, woodsy soil.	Bright yellow bark on twiggy stems in winter.

Comments: Similar in cultivation and soil needs to *Cornus alba* 'Sibirica', which has bright red bark on its young stems in winter.

	Zones	Height	Light	Soil	Highlights
Thuja occidentalis 'Ellwangeriana Aurea'	6–8	10 ft.	Full sun.	Moist, woodsy soil.	This evergreen has bright medium green foliage which turns bronzey green in winter.

Comments: 'Rheingold' is a more golden and improved form of the cultivar. In colder zones, substitute a golden juniper.

green foliage turns bronze in the winter. In areas colder than Zone 6, this cultivar can be browned or killed by low temperatures. But one of the shrubby, conical, bronze-to-gold junipers such as *Juniperus virginiana* var. *ellegantissima* would be a cold-hardy substitute. This bronze passage in the landscape harmonizes beautifully with the yellow dogwood.

The masterstroke is the smoldering fire of a stand of red Siberian dogwood (*Cornus alba* 'Sibirica') behind the arborvitae. The bronze tinge of the arborvitae is thus separated into its pure colors by the yellow and red dogwoods on either side. This is brilliant color planning at any time of the year, particularly in winter. You can keep this plant attractive by removing old wood, which is less showy, therebye encouraging the more brilliant red of the young shoots.

Good Background Plants

Selecting interesting and attractive background plants as focal points for the

Cornus alba 'Sibirica' and Chamaecyparus lawsoniana 'Winston Churchill' create strong winter interest, above. The striking orange branches of Salix alba var. viticella, shown with hellebores and bergenia, opposite top, will also make a dramatic show in the winter garden. A native of Siberia, Cornus alba 'Sibirica', opposite below, is hardy to subzero temperatures and looks beautiful with a light dusting of snow.

winter garden takes just a bit more imagination and concentration than for other seasons. Bushy heaths (*Erica* spp.), which provide a winter bloom of rosy-red flowers can provide additional interest, echoing the red dogwood. The ground cover 'Brightness,' a heather or the heath *Erica carnea* 'Springwood White' which is sometimes more readily available, would be good choices.

Heaths and heathers perform well in mild coastal areas, and especially the Pacific Northwest, but less well inland where the ground freezes to substantial depths. They prefer a sandy, well-drained, acidic soil; applications of azalea food may be necessary. They will not survive in heavy wet clays. The arborvitae and dogwoods are not as picky and will thrive in ordinary soil.

In areas unsuited for heaths and heathers, select one of the hardy, shiny-leaved groundcovers, such as *Cotoneaster horizontalis*, which also produces red fruit that echoes the Siberian dogwood. Or choose the rich dark green pachysandra if the area gets summer shade.

Though rather formal, this arrangement of plants is satisfying and full of life and interest in a season where little else may be happening. The use of the red and yellow dogwoods to harmonize with a winter-bronzed evergreen is a supremely useful idea throughout most of the country. Keep the two dogwoods separated, as they cancel each other out when planted together, losing much of their dramatic effect.

COAST SILKTASSEL & SPURGE

Garrya elliptica & Euphorbia characias var. *wulfenii*

Magical Forms Enliven the Winter Landscape

The winter garden of the far north may be a place of stone, cold, and silence. But plants that thrive in the more temperate climes—along the Atlantic coast through the Sun Belt to the West—sometimes choose winter for their best displays, and are enlivened by the frosts from the breath of the north wind.

There are a number of interesting plant forms for the winter garden, other than sculptural limbs and trunks discussed elsewhere, that can provide attractive displays during the winter months. Many broad-leaved evergreens persist in Zones 7 and 8—Japanese fatsia (*Fatsia japonica)* comes to mind, along with camellias and hellebores. Some produce fanciful shapes that can look like ice sculptures when covered in

Gardeners in the Sun Belt of the southern and western U.S. can plant the coast silktassel (Garrya elliptica) *and enjoy its long, icicle-like tassels on frosty mornings. Here it is paired with spurge* (Euphorbia characias *var.* wulfenii).

COAST SILKTASSEL & EUPHORBIA

	Zones	Height	Light	Soil	Highlights
Garrya elliptica	7	20 ft.	Partial to full sun.	Average well-drained soil.	Male catkins 3–8 in. long make a showy cascade in winter.

Comments: As an evergreen with many practical uses and great winter interest, coast silktassel is unsurpassed.

	Zones	Height	Light	Soil	Highlights
Euphorbia characias var. *wulfenii*	8	4 ft.	Full sun.	Average well-drained soil.	Makes mounds of yellow flower bracts in winter that last to summer.

Comments: This spurge also associates well with hydrangeas and geraniums (*Pelargonium* spp.*)*.

frost; combined, these plants make wonderful marriages for winter garden focal points.

Coast silktassel (*Garrya elliptica*), and a species of spurge (*Euphorbia characias* var. *wulfenii*) are good examples. The coast silktassel blooms with showy three- to eight-inch silky, male catkins in December to February, during the prime frost season.

The spurge's whirling, chartreuse columns make an excellent contrast with the vertical lines of the silktassel's catkins. This particular species produces a mass of four-foot evergreen stalks with regular patterns of blue-green leaves and rounded heads of yellowish green flower bracts from January into midspring. The puffy, green flower heads provide wintertime interest and are occasionally bowed with crowns of ice crystals. More often, flowering starts only after the midwinter frost season is over.

An evergreen with hollylike, wavy-edged, dark green leaves that are gray and woolly underneath, coast silktassel forms a shrub that reaches to twenty feet. It can be trained to cover a fence like a vine—a very practical use, as it screens off unwanted views twelve months of the year and provides such a great show when little else is happening. Pruned to a single trunk, coast silktassel will form a small tree; pruned to a bush shape, it will function as an evergreen shrub.

The male catkins of the coast silktassel are the longest and showiest. The female catkins are just a couple of inches long; they are followed by purple fruit that hangs on the plant all summer (unless eaten by birds). Both a male and female need to be present for the fruit to appear, but most gardeners plant only the male because it will produce the impressive catkins (which are the true interest).

The coast silktassel is a native of redwood country—the strip of coastal mountains and hills that extend from southern Oregon to California's central coast. Winters can be quite frosty in this region, especially at higher elevations, but not cold enough to permanently damage plants like silktassel or spurge.

The greenish-yellow flower bracts of spurge stay on the plant through the spring, holding their color until summer when the seeds ripen and the stalks yellow. They should be removed from the base then, allowing the younger stalks to grow to flowering size.

The spurge likes full sun, while the silktassel will take either full sun or partial shade. Both like a loose, well-drained soil and are somewhat tolerant of drought.

Be careful when handling spurge, as its acrid white sap is poisonous and an irritant to some people. The silktassel presents no such problems.

Other Winter-Blooming Plants

For areas colder than Zone 7, there are several interesting alternatives to coast silktassel for charming winter flowers. The very hardy Harry Lauder's walking stick (*Corylus avellana* 'Contorta'), has showy yellowish catkins in winter, but grows only to about four to six feet and is deciduous. The hardier members of the genus *Pieris* (sometimes called *Andromeda*), could also substitute. Many are not too much hardier than silktassel, but recent interest has lead to the cultivation of some species and cultivars hardy to Zone 4.

Although its flowers are a brighter yellow than the spurge's bracts, winter jasmine (*Jasminum nudiflorum*), hardy to Zone 6, makes an attractive fountain of yellow bloom in midwinter like the spurge. This jasmine's rounded shape would provide an interesting contrast with the silktassel's pendulous catkins.

*Harry Lauder's walking stick (*Coryllus avellana 'Contorta'), top, provides a fascinating alternative to the garrya for gardeners north of Zone 7. Garrya displays itself with an evergreen chamaecyparus for a lovely winter scene, bottom. Opposite, Eleagnus ebbingei 'Gilt Edge' is an evergreen for the winter garden whose red berries, incidentally, make a good jelly.*

HELLEBORE & BRAMBLE

Helleborus foetidus & Rubus cockburnianus

An Appreciation of Winter Textures

In late winter, before the crocuses bloom, much of the garden is locked up in ice or is turning into a muddy quagmire. It is decorated with little other than the frost-blasted detritus of last season's herbaceous growth. For most people it is a bleak time, best spent indoors. What a treat, then, to find some signs of life and artful combinations of plants that look best at this time of year.

Tall, gracefully arching canes of brambles (*Rubus cockburnianus*) are a good place to start when choosing an association for late winter. This bramble is particularly pretty because of the light mauve or purplish-gray waxy bloom on its canes. And when hardly anything else is even poking its head up—let alone blooming—the hellebores (*Helleborus foetidus*) are up and setting out their flowers and evergreen leaves.

Helleborus foetidus—it has no common name that I know of, but the Latin translates to "stinking hellebore"—is a strange, bravely hardy little plant that chooses the last half of winter, from February to April, to bloom. The flowers, like those of most others in its genus, are shy and face downward, which gives

	Zones	Height	Light	Soil	Highlights
HELLEBORE & BRAMBLE					
Helleborus foetidus	4	18 in.	Full to shade.	Rich, moist soil.	Flowers from February to April with shy, nodding green cups; dark green leathery leaves

Comments: *H. foetidus* self-sows. Also nice is the Lenten rose *Helleborus orientalis*, with greenish-whitish-mauve to rose flowers.

	Zones	Height	Light	Soil	Highlights
Rubus cockburnianus	7	6 ft.	Full sun.	Average moist soil.	Waxy, gray to purplish canes make an interesting show in winter.

Comments: Similar effects with winter canes can be achieved with commercial fruiting blackberries—with the additional bonus of the summer fruit.

the plant rounded appearance, like clusters of green balls above masses of attractive, very dark green, divided leaves held in elegant tiers. Ignoring frosts and cold, damp weather, snows, and ice storms, the hellebore opens its clusters of lime green cups at the first hints of the return of the far-off spring sun.

Combining them with a stand of bare bramble canes makes an excellent marriage of contrasting textures; the hellebore's soft, smooth flowers are set off by the prickly shafts of the bramble canes. The combination also features interesting contrasts of forms (leafy, flowering hellebores against bare upright brambles), and colors (the hellebores' greens against the brambles' subtly colored canes).

To do their best, hellebores like shade or partial shade, and rich, compost-amended soil and constant moisture, although they will persist during dry spells. The same kind of rich soil is favored by the brambles.

Brambles like partial shade to full sun, so the site for this marriage will

*An interesting collection of contrasting textures is created in this marriage of the bold, upright, skeletal canes of a bramble (*Rubus cockburnianus*) and the warm textured, winter-flowering hellebore (*Helleborus foetidus*).*

A Gallery of Bramble Fruits

The genus *Rubus* contains some of the most luscious berries in the world. And fortunately, some of the best-tasting varieties have the upright canes needed to create a marriage with hellebores. Here are some selections that would be appropriate:

'Thornless Evergreen' or 'Thornfree' blackberries are widely adapted to the western U.S. They are heavy-fruiting sorts with semi-erect thornless canes to 6-8 feet. Certainly they are easier to deal with than most blackberries carrying wicked thorns.

'Brazos,' 'Comanche,' and 'Rosborough' are erect blackberries suited to Zones 7-9.

In the very cold winter climates of north, the best and sweetest blackberries are those with an erect habit, including 'Darrow' and 'Illini Hardy.'

In Zones 6-8, erect blackberry cultivars with exceptional berries are 'Cherokee,' 'Choctaw,' 'Cheyenne,' 'Navaho Thornless', and 'Shawnee'.

Among raspberries, 'Kilarney' is a good summer-bearing red with strong canes; 'Redwing' is a very hardy red raspberry that bears in fall; 'Cumberland' and 'Jewel' are among the best black raspberries; 'Royalty' is an excellent purple raspberry; 'Fallgold' is the choice fall-bearing yellow raspberry, and wineberry (*Rubus phoenocolasius*) is a raspberrylike summer-bearing fruit with reddish-brown, semi-erect canes and a preference for light shade and moist, rich soil.

*The white canes of another bramble (*Rubus biflorus*) provide a stark contrast in texture and form to the hardy, orange-flowered witch hazel (*Hamamelis × intermedia 'Jelena'*) in this very striking winter garden pairing, opposite. A hellebore and cotoneaster pairing provides an exquisite composition of texture, overleaf.*

have to be a compromise between the sun-loving brambles and the shade-loving hellebores: a spot with good morning sun (but afternoon shade would be fine.)

The bramble forms clumps that need yearly maintenance. Its canes are biennial and grow to size in the first year. Some species fruit the first fall, then again in the next spring on the same canes, which then die back. Other species produce only foliage on first-year canes, then fruit the following year, before dying back. In either case, canes need to be pruned out at soil level after fruiting. First-fall fruiters can be cut back during their first winter, or after they have given some early season berries. Second-year fruiters should be cut back during the following dormant season. New ones will appear in the spring to replace them.

Other Choices

Other species of *Helleborus* can substitute for *H. foetidus*. The Lenten rose (*H. orientalis*), green suffused with purple, mauve, or rose, might accentuate the brambles even more than *H. foetidus*—colors that would harmonize with the waxy, gray-purple bramble canes. The Lenten rose blooms a bit later than *H. foetidus*, however, which would cut into the time when it could effectively associate with dormant bramble canes, which leaf out early in temperate climates.

The season for this marriage might be extended by substituting the Christmas rose (*Helleborus niger*). *The Christmas rose* begins blooming in December in milder zones—February to March in the colder parts of its range—with white to greenish white flowers that darken to a purplish mauve with age. It has dark leaves like *H. foetidus*.

R. cockburnianus is a relatively rare bramble species, but any of your favorite upright, cane-forming blackberries or raspberries can substitute. One of the commercial black raspberries such as 'Cumberland' or 'Jewel' would be ideal. Among the brambles, *Rubus phoenocolasius*—the wineberry—tolerates partial to full shade the best. Perhaps the closest ornamental bramble in appearance to *R. cockburnianus* is a Himalayan blackberry (*Rubus biflorus*) that may be easier to find.

Keep brambles within set boundaries, or their underground spreading roots will have them coming up in the hellebores (or any other groundcover with which has been chosen to surround them). The hellebores also look nice mixed with early bloomers, such as daffodils, primroses (*Primula*), violets, and evergreens, like rhododendrons, and ferns.

H. foetidus is a rapid spreader, and freely self-sows where it likes its spot. Thus it is easier to establish in a large bed than either of the other hellebores. For a large patch to surround the bramble, *H. foetidus* is the most practical choice, even if the Lenten rose is perhaps prettier.

CHAPTER FOUR

CULTURAL CONSIDERATIONS

No matter how much attention you pay to design and placement, a plant marriage will not succeed if it is not suited to both the climate and the specific conditions of the site (soil makeup, water availability and the amount and quality of sunlight and shade). Partners in a marriage must share similar needs. Clearly, there would be little point in pairing a plant that likes full sun and poor, dry soil, such as one of the sedums, with one that thrives in full shade and rich, moist soil, like an astilbe. One or both will suffer.

Hardiness

If you are not sure whether or not a plant is suited to your particular location, you can consult the United States Hardiness Zone Map (see pages 162–163), which is produced by the United States Department of Agriculture. Divided into eleven zones, the map indicates the average minimum temperature in each, enabling you to check if plants will live through the winter in your region of the country.

These guidelines, however, do not account for the many variables that may affect plant hardiness, such as rainfall, humidity, wind exposure, summer heat, soil mixtures, moisture levels, and light intensity. There is a world of difference, for example, between the humid Zone 9 in southern Louisiana and the drier Zone 9 in California, where it hardly rains at all between May and October. Moreover, in some areas of the same zone, such as near the coastline or a forest, climatic conditions can differ substantially within a few square miles.

Use the U.S.D.A. Zone Map as a general guide to optimum growing conditions, and take into account your property's microclimates. In the same garden, the area in front of a south-facing rock wall, for instance, will be much warmer in winter than a spot on a shady northwestern slope exposed to prevailing winter winds.

Sunlight and Shade

The partners in a plant marriage must have compatible light requirements, but that does not necessarily mean that they need the same amount of sun. A good marriage can also occur when one plant helps satisfy the needs of another: shrubs and perennials that favor partial sun, such as cardinal flowers (*Lobelia cardinalis*) and mountain laurels (*Kalmia latifolia*), for example, will both benefit when planted in the shade of large sun-loving lilacs.

Sun-loving plants simply will not tolerate full shade,

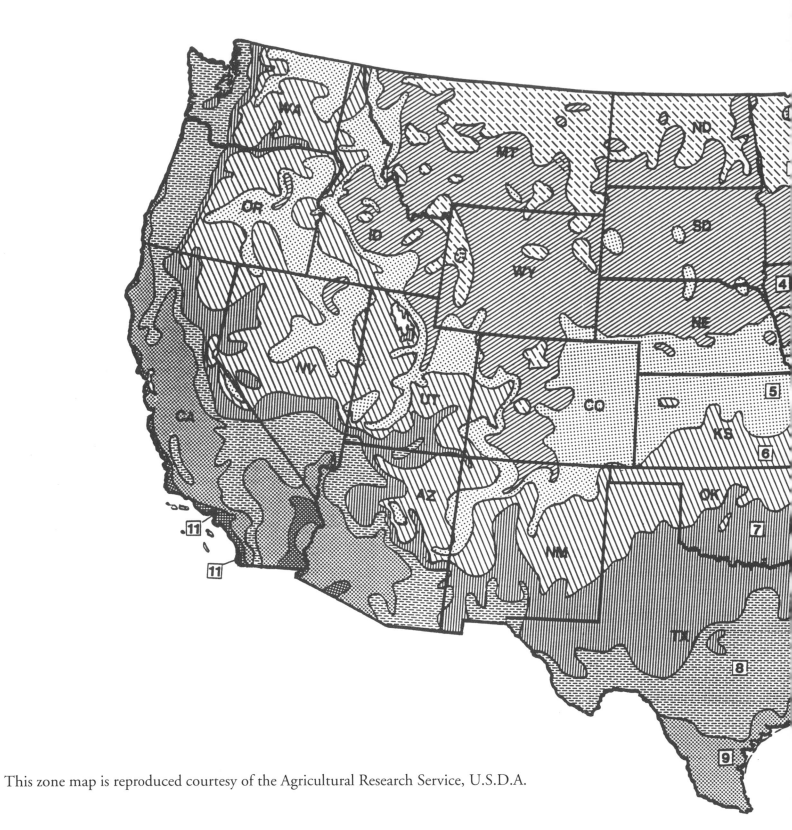

This zone map is reproduced courtesy of the Agricultural Research Service, U.S.D.A.

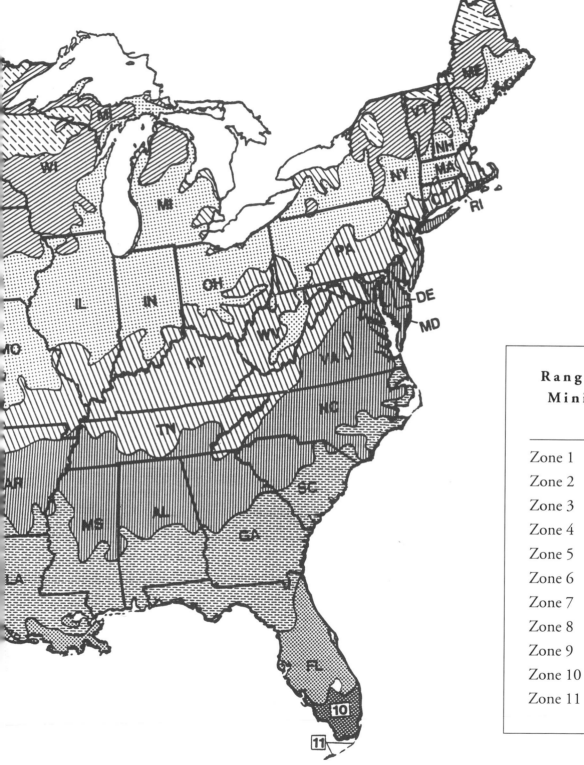

Range of Average Annual Minimum Temperatures for Each Zone

Zone 1	Below −50°F	
Zone 2	−50° to −40°F	
Zone 3	−40° to −30°F	
Zone 4	−30° to −20°F	
Zone 5	−20° to −10°F	
Zone 6	−10° to 0°F	
Zone 7	0° to 10°F	
Zone 8	10° to 20°F	
Zone 9	20° to 30°F	
Zone 10	30° to 40°F	
Zone 11	Above 40°F	

although they may get by on partial sun. Shade-lovers, in turn, will suffer and die under the blasting rays of the direct sun. For any other conditions—dappled sunlight, bright shade, or intermittent sun and shade over the course of a day—your own intuition and best guesses must come into play.

Assume, however, that most plants will accept light shade or sun for just part of the day. And remember that light conditions also change from east to west and north to south. Full sun in the Arizona desert is vastly different from full sun in Maine.

Some plants are very forgiving, tolerating an enormous variation in climate and conditions, and thus make safe, easy-going choices for marriages. The star jasmine (*Trachelospermum jasminoides*) accepts whatever it finds: rich soil/poor soil; full sun/full shade; wet humus or dry sand. The common—and invasive—goutweed (*Aegopodium podagraria*) will also tolerate practically any light conditions.

Soil

The ideal garden soil consists of equal parts sand, silt and clay, amended with as much organic matter as possible. As the vast numbers of microorganisms—tiny animals and bacteria—that live in the soil dismantle the organic matter, it turns into humus, a crumbly, dark, rich substance that holds water-soluble nutrients until plants call for them. A humus-rich soil (which most plants prefer), stays moist longer, is replete with nutrients, and promotes good drainage.

Soil pH, another consideration, is the measurement of the acidity of any given soil. The term "pH" refers to the concentration of hydrogen ions in a solution and is measured on a scale from 0 to 14, in which 7 is neutral. The lower the number below 7, the more acidic the solution; the higher the number above 7, the more alkaline. Roots can take up nutrients only after they are dissolved in the soil solution; in very acidic or alkaline soils, nutrients remain locked up in insoluble forms and are unavailable to plants. (Nitrogen, phosphorus, and potassium are the most important plant nutrients, but over a dozen others are needed in much smaller amounts.)

The greatest number of essential nutrients become soluble and available to the majority of plants at a slightly acidic pH. Thus, most plants prefer a pH between 6.0 and 6.5. Of course, there are exceptions. Grasses, for example, prefer slightly alkaline, or "sweet," soil. Bog plants, many conifers, and rhododendrons, on the other hand, prefer a distinctly acidic soil and would not do well in an alkaline one.

If you do not know the pH measurement of your soil, you can have it tested by a laboratory for a small fee. If the pH level needs adjusting, the lab report will indicate what you should add to the soil.

Only adjust your soil's pH level if it tests very acidic or very alkaline. Otherwise, you are much better off simply adding compost and organic matter to the soil regularly. The pH of soil heavily amended with organic matter will naturally tend toward 6.5.

Usually, the different partners in a plant marriage will take up nutrients differently. One likes more potassium and phosphorus, perhaps, while another favors more nitrogen and manganese. Soil that is healthy and alive, with plenty of organic matter can supply each partner with the nutrients it requires.

Water

One of the chief causes of poor plant performance is the lack of adequate moisture. When plants do not get enough water, their leaf and flower production is curtailed and they become weak and spindly. On the other hand, standing water—indicating poor drainage—will kill many plants.

Moisture requirements, of course, change with the plant: yuccas, for instance, need much less water than a stand of Virginia bluebells (*Mertensia virginica*). Fortunately, most plants prefer the same thing: a loamy, well-drained soil that is always moist but never wet. In many northern parts of the country, natural rainfall supplies most of the water needed for ornamental plantings. Other regions are more arid—including the desert areas west of the Rockies and California's semi-desert—and therefore require irrigation. But even in regions of heavy rainfall, some form of irrigation is usually necessary during the summer months.

When watering your garden, use a type of drip irrigation, if you can—such as soaker hoses—rather than overhead sprinklers. Soaker hoses allow moisture to seep directly into the soil just where it is needed and use a minimum of water. Overhead watering, on the other hand, wets leaves, promoting mildew, and can ruin ornamental flowers. Peonies, for example, turn to brown mush when soaked by sprinklers. If you must water with a sprinkler, do it in the morning so the leaves are dry before sundown.

Watering can be kept to minimum by amending the soil with plenty of actively decaying organic matter—which turns into moisture-retaining humus—and by mulching with organic materials such as hay, pine needles or shredded leaves. The mulch smothers weeds and prevents the soil from drying out. Later, as it decays, it produces nutrients and eventually turns into humus as well.

Plants that prefer boggy conditions, such as water flag (*Iris pseudacorus*), sweet flag (*Acorus calamus*) or common scouring rush (*Equisetum hyemale*), can be grouped in poorly-drained areas. Those that prefer dry soils, such as Mediterranean herbs and shrubs, including rosemary, ceanothus and some California natives like manzanita, will do well on top of berms or mounded soil that dries out quickly.

What Else is Growing on the Site?

Certain plants have an allelopathic effect on their neighbors, producing chemicals that inhibit the growth of nearby plants. Black walnut trees (*Juglans nigra*) are well-known producers of allelopathic substances, found in their leaves and nut rinds; many plants grow poorly, if at all, underneath their canopies. Black locusts (*Robinia pseudoacacia*) and dense evergreens also have similar allelopathic effects, as do some tall perennial grasses, which produce allelopathic compounds in their roots, particularly buffalo grass (*Buchloe dactyloides*) and bermuda grass (*Cynodon dactylon*).

Tangled tree roots near the soil surface are another, more common, danger to plant marriages. Be wary of siting a marriage under the dripline of a large tree. Just under the soil, its roots are already grabbing the lion's share of water and nutrients, ready to choke out anything planted near them. If you must plant near trees, choose woodland plants that associate naturally with big trees, such as black snakeroot (*Cimicifuga racemosa*), or simply keep plantings far enough from the trunks so that the tree roots will not interfere with their growth.

Acidity, too, can be a problem. The soil under evergreens usually has a very low pH, for instance, and is best suited to acid-loving plants like rhododendrons. Otherwise, you need to amend it with ground limestone to sweeten it.

Pests and Diseases

When making a marriage, try not to put plants together that are prone to the same pests and diseases. For instance, grapes and roses each attract Japanese beetles; together they would be all but irresistible to these plant-eating insects. Similarly, both roses and garden phlox (*Phlox paniculata*) are prone to powdery mildew, so it is best to keep these plants apart.

Learn which diseases and insect pests are likely to bother the plants you are considering. If there is overlap, look for a non-susceptible substitute for one of the plants. You should also find out which diseases and insect pests are particularly prevalent in your region, and avoid any plants that are bothered by them.

Healthy plants—those that are "thrifty"—or robust and growing at the right size and speed—are apt to be more resistant to disease and insects than sickly ones. Plants that appear sick or weak may be a warning that the soil is poor, which can be rectified by improving the soil with the addition of compost or other organic matter. If a plant is constantly under attack by a pest or disease, remove it altogether. Why keep it in the garden? There are so many choices of plants that you certainly do not have to keep one that has problems.

RESOURCES

These suppliers were selected for the quality of their merchandise, their range of plants, helpful service and knowledgeable staff. Each entry includes a current mailing address, and in some cases a street address for those wishing to visit the supplier. Readers are also encouraged to seek out local nurseries and suppliers, who are likely to be well-informed as to the best plants for the area.

GENERAL SUPPLIES

W. Atlee Burpee & Co.
Warminster, PA 18974
All types of seed. Also plants, bulbs and supplies.

Gardener's Supply Co.
128 Intervale Road
Burlington, VT 05401
Equipment, including a range of greenhouses, and tools.

Harmony Farm Supply
P.O. Box 460
Graton, CA 95444
Equipment, including home irrigation systems, and tools.

Johnny's Selected Seeds
Foss Hill Road
Albion, ME 04910
Garden supplies and seeds.

Milaeger's Gardens
4838 Douglas Avenue
Racine, WI 53402-2498
Garden supplies, perennials, vines and roses.

Walt Nicke Co.
P.O. Box 433
36 McLeod Lane
Topsfield, MA 01983
Interesting and hard-to-find tools and gardening equipment.

Stokes Seeds, Inc.
Box 548
Buffalo, NY 14240-0548
All types of seeds and garden supplies.

Wayside Gardens
One Garden Lane
Hodges, SC 29695
Plants, bulbs, shrubs and trees.

White Flower Farm
Litchfield, CT 06759-0050
Select perennials, shrubs and bulbs.

BULBS

B & D Lilies
330 P Street
Port Townsend, WA 98368
Hybrid and species lilies.

Breck's
U.S. Reservation Center
6523 North Galena Road
Peoria, IL 61656
Spring- and summer-blooming bulbs.

Cascade Daffodils
1790 Richard Circle
West St. Paul, MN 55118-3821
Standard and miniature daffodils.

Daffodil Mart
Route 3, Box 794
Gloucester, VA 23061
Daffodils and other spring-blooming bulbs.

Dutch Gardens, Inc.
P.O. Box 200
Adelphia, NJ 07710
Spring and summer-blooming bulbs.

Honeywood Lilies
P.O. Box 63
Parkside, SK
Canada S0J 2A0
Lilies, tulips, alliums, irises and peonies.

Jackson & Perkins
60 Rose Lane
Medford, OR 97501
Summer- and fall-blooming varieties.

Peter de Jager Bulb Co.
P.O. Box 2010
188 Asbury Street
South Hamilton, MA 01982
Spring- and fall-blooming bulbs.

McClure & Zimmerman
108 W. Winnebago
P.O. Box 368
Friesland, WI 53935
*Species tulips, bulbous irises and
unusual summer-flowering bulbs,
including alliums.*

Grant Mitsch Novelty Dafffodils
P.O. Box 218
Hubbard, OR 97032
Unusual daffodil hybrids.

Netherland Bulb Co., Inc.
13 McFadden Road
Easton, PA 18042
*Spring- and summer-flowering
bulbs.*

Quality Dutch Bulbs
P.O. Box 225
50 Lake Drive
Hillsdale, NJ 07642
Large variety of Dutch bulbs.

Smith & Hawken
25 Corte Madera
Mill Valley, CA 94941
*Tulips, crocuses, daffodils, and
other spring bloomers, as well as
lilies, some daylilies and irises.*

Van Bourgondien Bros.
P.O. Box A
245 Farmingdale Road
Babylon, NY 11702
*Spring- and summer-flowering
bulbs and perennials.*

Van Engelen, Inc.
Stillbrook Farm
313 Maple Street
Litchfield, CT 06759
Dutch bulbs, including lilies.

The Waushara Gardens
Rt. 2, Box 570
Plainfield, WI 54966
Summer-blooming bulbs.

GROUNDCOVERS AND VINES

The Fragrant Path
P.O. Box 328
Fort Calhoun, NE 68023
*Seeds for scented vines,
perennials and annuals.*

Gilson Gardens
P.O. Box 277
3059 U.S. Route 20
Perry, OH 44081
*Groundcovers, perennials
and vines.*

Clematis

D.S. George Nurseries
2515 Penfield Road
Fairport, NY 14450
A large selection of clematis.

Steffan's Clematis
P.O. Box 184
1259 Fairport Road
Fairport, NY 14450
Large selection of clematis.

Grasses and Ferns

Kurt Bluemel, Inc.
2740 Greene Lane
Baldwin, MD 21013-9523
*Ornamental grasses, sedges,
bamboos, ferns, perennials
and groundcovers.*

Fancy Fronds
1911 4th Avenue West
Seattle, WA 98119
Wide selection of hardy ferns.

Greenlee Nursery
301 E. Franklin Avenue
Pomona, CA 91766
*Ornamental grasses, rushes
and sedges.*

Limerock Ornamental
  Grasses, Inc.
R.D. 1, Box 111-C
Port Matilda, PA 16870
Bareroot and container grasses.

Heaths and Heathers

Heaths and Heathers
P.O. Box 850
Elma, WA 98541
Over 100 varieties.

Hedgehog Hill Farm
RFD 2, Box 2010
Buckfield, ME 04220
*Herbs, perennials, annuals and
vegetables.*

Rock Spray Nursery
Box 693
Truro, MA 02666
Broad selection of heathers.

PERENNIALS

Bluestone Perennials, Inc.
7211 Middle Road
Madison, OH 44057
Wide selection of perennials.

Busse Gardens
Route 2, Box 238
Cokato, MN 55321-9426
*A selection of unusual
perennials.*

Carroll Gardens
P.O. Box 310
444 East Main Street
Westminster, MD 21157
*Perennials, herbs, wildflowers,
ferns, grasses, bulbs, rock-
garden plants, shrubs and trees.*

Milaeger's Gardens
4838 Douglas Avenue
Racine, WI 53402-2498
Perennials, vines and roses.

Oliver Nursuries, Inc.
1159 Bronson Road
Fairfield, CT 06430
Perennials, wildflowers, alpine plants, trees, shrubs, groundcovers and vines.

Perpetual Perennials
1111 Upper Valley Pike
Springfield, OH 45504
Wildflowers, grasses and dried flowers.

André Viette Farm and Nursery
Route 1, Box 16
Fishersville, VA 22939
Unusual perennials, hostas, daylilies, poppies, peonies and iris.

Daylilies and Irises

American Daylily &
Perennials
P.O. Box 210
Grain Valley, MO 64029
Daylilies, some cannas, peonies and perennials.

Lee Bristol Nursery
Bloomfields Farm
Gaylordsville, CT 06755-0005
Wide range of daylilies.

Busse Gardens
Route 2, Box 238
Cokato, MN 55321
Wide range of daylilies and irises.

Comanche Acres Iris Gardens
RR-I, Box 258
Gower, MI 64454
Large selection of bearded irises.

Geraniums

Cook's Geranium Nursery
712 N. Grand
Lyons, KS 67554
Dwarfs, species, ivy-leaved, scented and zonal geraniums.

Merry Gardens
P.O. Box 595
Camden, ME 04843
Geraniums, ivies and rare plants.

Wheeler Farm Gardens
171 Bartlett Street
Portland, CT 06480
Zonal and ivy geraniums.

Hostas

The Crownsville Nursery
P.O. Box 797
Crownsville, MD 21032
Ferns, hostas, grasses and woody plants.

Savory's Gardens, Inc.
5300 Whiting Avenue
Edina, MN 55439-1249
Broad range of hostas.

Peonies

Caprice Farm Nursery
15425 S.W. Pleasant Hill Road
Sherwood, OR 97140
Peonies, daylilies, hostas and Japanese and Siberian irises.

Tischler Peony Garden
1021 E. Division Street
Faribault, MN 55021
Single, double, Japanese and hybrid peonies.

SEEDS

Abundant Life
P.O. Box 772
Port Townsend, WA 98368
Open-pollinated seeds for vegetables, herbs, flowers, small grains, trees and shrubs.

W. Atlee Burpee & Co.
Warminster, PA 18974
All types of seed.

The Fragrant Path
P.O. Box 328
Fort Calhoun, NE 68023
Seeds for old-fashioned, scented flowers.

Nichols Garden Nursery
1190 North Pacific Highway
Albany, OR 97321-4598
Vegetable, herb and flower seeds.

Park Seed Company, Inc.
Cokesbury Road
Greenwood, SC 29647-0001
All types of seed.

Pinetree Garden Seeds
New Gloucester, ME 04260
Over 600 varieties of flower, herb and culinary seeds.

The Redwood City Seed
Company
P.O. Box 361
Redwood City, CA 94064
Old-fashioned seed varieties.

Seeds Blüm
Idaho City Stage
Boise, ID 83706
Wide range of vegetable and flower seed.

Shepherd's Garden Seeds
6116 Highway 9
Felton, CA 95018
Gourmet vegetables, culinary herbs, unusual and edible flowers.

Stokes Seeds, Inc.
Box 548
Buffalo, NY 14240-0548
All types of seeds.

Territorial Seed Co.
P.O. Box 157
20 Palmer Avenue
Cottage Grove, OR 97424
Wide seed selection, particularly vegetables for West Coast.

Thompson & Morgan
P.O. Box 1308
Jackson, NJ 08527
Seeds for all common and rare flowering plants; perennials, annuals, vegetables and trees.

Wall Sweep Herb Farm
317 Mt. Bethel Road
Port Murray, NJ 07865
Unusual plants.

William Dam Seeds
P.O. Box 8400
Dundas, Ontario, Canada
L9H 6M1
Vegetable, flower and vine seeds.

TREES AND SHRUBS

Ahrens Nursery and Plant Lab
RRI Box FN 89
Huntingberg, IN 47542
Berries, fruits and herbs.

Arrowhead Nursery
Watia Road, Box 38
Bryson City, NC 28713
*Rare native ornamentals
including dogwoods and
magnolias.*

Bluestone Perennials, Inc.
7211 Middle Road
Madison, OH 44057
*Wide selection of shrubs
and perennials.*

Carino Nurseries
Box 538
Indiana, PA 15701
*Ornamental seedlings and
transplants, deciduous trees
and shrubs.*

Carroll Gardens
P.O. Box 310
444 East Main Street
Westminster, MD 21157
*Perennials, herbs, wildflowers,
ferns, grasses, bulbs, rock garden plants, shrubs and trees.*

Champlain Isle Argo
Associates
Isle La Motte, VT 05463
*Unusual ornamental shrubs
and shade trees, as well as
berries and grapes.*

Forest Farm
990 Tetherow Road
Williams, OR 97544-9599
*Unusual shrubs and trees,
including many native
varieties.*

Foxborough Nursery, Inc.
3611 Miller Road
Street, MD 21154
*Dwarf and unusual conifers,
broadleafs and other trees.*

Girard Nurseries
P.O. Box 428
Geneva, OH 44041-0428
*Azaleas, rhododendrons, dwarf
evergreens, conifers and rare
trees and shrubs.*

Gossler Farms Nursery
1200 Weaver Road
Springfield, OR 97478-9691
*Unusual shrubs and trees and
magnolias.*

Greer Gardens
1280 Goodpasture Island Road
Eugene, OR 97401-1794
*Unusual rhododendrons,
azaleas, camellias, conifers
and ornamental trees.*

Hollyvale Farm
Box 69
Humptulips, WA 98552
*Wide variety of unusual land-
scape hollies and cultivars.*

Louk's Nursery
P.O. Box 102
Cloverdale, OR 97112
Unusual Japanese maples.

Malvern Nursery
Box 265 B, Route 2
Asheville, NC 28805
Ornamental plants.

Miniature Plant Kingdom
4125 Harrison Grade Road
Sebastopol, CA 95472
*Dwarf conifers, ornamental
trees and shrubs.*

Mountain Maples
5901 Spy Rock Road
Laytonville, CA 95454-1329
*Japanese maples and dwarf
conifers.*

Oikos Tree Crops
721 North Fletcher
Kalamazoo, MI 49007-3077
*Native oaks (species and hybrid),
nut trees, native fruit trees
and unusual ornamentals.*

Plants of The Southwest
Agua Fria
Rt. 6, Box 11-A
Santa Fe, NM 87501
*Perennials, herbs, grasses (both
plants and seeds), shrubs and
wildflowers for the Southwest.*

Roslyn Nursery
211 Burrs Lane
Dix Hills, NY 11746
*Rhododendrons, azaleas,
hollies, laurels, rare trees
and evergreens.*

Springvale Farm Nursery
Mozier Hollow Road
Hamburg, IL 62045
*Dwarf, rare and unusual trees,
shrubs and conifers, deciduous
trees and rock-garden plants.*

Transplant Nursery
Parkertown Road
Lavonia, GA 30553
*Native and evergreen azaleas
and rhododendrons.*

Twombly Nursery, Inc.
163 Barn Hill Road
Monroe, CT 06468
*Rare and unusual trees, shrubs,
ferns and ornamental grasses.*

Valley Nursery
Box 4845
Helena, MT 59601
*Ornamental trees, conifers
and shrubs.*

Washington Evergreen Nursery
P.O. Box 388
Brooks Branch Road
Leicester, NC 28748
*Dwarf conifers and mountain
laurels.*

Weston Nurseries
P.O. Box 186
Route 135
Hopkinton, MA 01748
*Landscape-size trees, shrubs,
perennials, flowers and fruits.*

White Flower Farm
Litchfield, CT 06759
*Bulbs, flowering perennials
and shrubs.*

Woodlanders
1128 Colleton Avenue
Aiken, SC 29801
Native trees, shrubs and perennials.

Roses

The Antique Rose Emporium
Rt. 5, Box 143
Brenham, TX 77833
Old-fashioned roses.

Heirloom Roses
24062 Riverside Drive NE
St. Paul, OR 97137
*Own-root roses, including old
garden roses and miniatures.*

Historical Roses
1657 W. Jackson St.
Painesville, OH 44077
Old-fashioned garden roses.

Jackson & Perkins
P.O. Box 1028
Medford, OR 97501
*Garden roses, perennials
and shrubs.*

Roses of Yesterday and Today
802 Brown's Valley Road
Watsonville, CA 95976
*Old, rare and select
modern roses.*

Spring Hill Select Roses
110 West Elm Street
Ripp City, OH 45371
Modern roses.

WATER GARDENS

Lilypons Water Gardens
P.O. Box 10
6800 Lilypons Road
Buckeystown, MD 21717
*Everything for the water
garden.*

Van Ness Water Gardens
2460 North Euclid Avneue
Upland, CA 91768
Water lilies and pond supplies.

INDEX

The most important plants suggested for pairings are indexed below by botanical name, and cross–referenced by common name. Each marriage is also listed by its defining characteristic.

BIBLIOGRAPHY

Beales, Peter. *Roses*. New York: Henry Holt and Co., 1992.

Cox, Jeff and Marilyn Cox. *Flowers for All Seasons*. Emmaus, PA: Rodale Press, 1987.

Cox, Jeff and Marilyn Cox. *The Perennial Garden*. Emmaus, PA: Rodale Press, 1985.

Heriteau, Jacqueline. *The National Arboretum Book of Outstanding Garden Plants*. New York: Simon & Schuster, 1990.

Jefferson-Brown, Michael. *Leaves*. London: David & Charles Publishers, 1989.

Liberty Hyde Bailey Hortorium, Staff of the. *Hortus Third*. Ithaca, NY: Cornell University Press, 1976.

Lloyd, Christopher. *Clematis*. Deer Park, WI: Capability's Books, 1989.

Phillips, Roger and Martyn Rix. *The Random House Book of Perennials*, Vols. 1 & 2. New York: Random House, 1991.

Phillips, Roger and Martyn Rix. *The Random House Book of Shrubs*. New York: Random House, 1989.

Sunset Books and Magazine, Editors of. *Western Garden Book*. Menlo Park, CA: Lane Publishing Co., 1988.

PHOTOGRAPHY CREDITS

1: Steven Wooster/The Garden Picture Library
2: Marijke Heuff/The Garden Picture Library
4: Ron Sutherland/The Garden Picture Library
6: Clive Nichols
8–9: Noel Kavanagh/The Garden Picture Library
10: Cynthia Woodyard
12: Andrew Lawson
14: Clive Nichols
15: Cynthia Woodyard
16: Didier Willery/The Garden Picture Library (top) Clive Nichols (bottom)
17: Tommy Candler/The Garden Picture Library
18: Andrew Lawson (top) Gary Rogers/The Garden Picture Library (bottom)
19: Andrew Lawson
20: Lamontagne/The Garden Picture Library
21: John Glover/The Garden Picture Library
22: Clive Nichols
23: Clive Nichols
24: Roger Hyam/The Garden Picture Library
27: Clive Nichols
30: Lamontagne/The Garden Picture Library
34: Ron Sutherland/The Garden Picture Library
35: Brigitte Thomas/The Garden Picture Library
36: Brian Carter/The Garden Picture Library

37: Brigitte Thomas/The Garden Picture Library
39: Brigitte Thomas/The Garden Picture Library
40: Clive Nichols
41: Clive Nichols
43: John Glover/The Garden Picture Library
44: Brigitte Thomas/The Garden Picture Library
45: Clive Nichols
47: Clive Nichols
48: Andrew Lawson
49: Clive Nichols
51: Cynthia Woodyard
52: Jerry Pavia (top) Andrew Lawson (bottom)
53: Andrew Lawson
55: Brigitte Thomas/The Garden Picture Library
56: Elvin McDonald
57: Andrew Lawson
59: Clive Nichols
60: Clive Nichols
61: Jacqui Hurst
62: Clive Nichols
63: Ron Sutherland/The Garden Picture Library
65: Clive Nichols
67: Clive Nichols
68: Andrew Lawson
69: Clive Nichols
71: Marijke Heuff/The Garden Picture Library
72: Marijke Heuff/The Garden Picture Library
73: Steven Wooster/The Garden Picture Library
74: Clive Nichols

77: Clive Nichols
78: Clive Nichols
80: Clive Nichols/The Garden Picture Library
81: Didier Willery/The Garden Picture Library
83: Jerry Pavia
84: Andrew Lawson
85: Steven Wooster/The Garden Picture Library
86: Clive Nichols
88: Brigitte Thomas/The Garden Picture Library
89: Saxon Holt
91: Steven Wooster/The Garden Picture Library
92: Brian Carter/The Garden Picture Library
93: Andrew Lawson
95: Cynthia Woodyard
97: Andrew Lawson
98–9: Cynthia Woodyard
100: Cynthia Woodyard
101: Andrew Lawson
103: Clive Nichols
104: Clive Nichols
105: Didier Willery/The Garden Picture Library
107: Clive Nichols
108: Clive Nichols
111: Jerry Pavia
112–3: Andrew Lawson
115: Clive Nichols
116: Clive Nichols
117: J. S. Sira/The Garden Picture Library
119: Clive Nichols
120–1: Andrew Lawson
123: Clive Nichols

124: Clive Nichols
125: Lauren Springer
127: Jacqui Hurst
128: Mick Hales
129: Clive Nichols
130: Clive Nichols
132: Cynthia Woodyard
133: Andrew Lawson
135: Cynthia Woodyard
136: Marijke Heuff/The Garden Picture Library
137: Clive Nichols
138: Clive Nichols
139: Brigitte Thomas/The Garden Picture Library
141: Didier Willery/The Garden Picture Library
142: J. S. Sira/The Garden Picture Library
143: John Glover/The Garden Picture Library
144: Clive Nichols
146: Andrew Lawson
146–7: John Glover/The Garden Picture Library
149: Clive Nichols
150–1: Clive Nichols
152: Clive Nichols
154: Andrew Lawson (top) Brian Carter/The Garden Picture Library (bottom)
155: Andrew Lawson
157: Clive Nichols
158: Clive Nichols
160: Clive Nichols

ACKNOWLEDGMENTS

I would like to acknowledge the contributions of the following people: Marilyn Cox for the original inspiration for this book; Charles de Kay for his support and cogent observations; Ruth Lively for her editorial help; John Smallwood for his determination to produce the best book possible; Dirk Kaufman for his stunning book design; Terri Hardin for her thorough copyediting of the manuscript; Susanna Napierala for her support and understanding throughout the project; and M. S. Wyeth, Jr. for his initial support for the book.